LITTLE PEOPLE
LITTLE PATRIOTS

LITTLE PEOPLE
LITTLE PATRIOTS

Saving America One Child at a Time

Steve Brezenski

authorHOUSE®

AuthorHouse™
1663 Liberty Drive
Bloomington, IN 47403
www.authorhouse.com
Phone: 1-800-839-8640

First published by AuthorHouse   10/28/2009

ISBN: 978-1-4490-3568-6 (e)
ISBN: 978-1-4490-3570-9 (sc)
ISBN: 978-1-4490-3569-3 (hc)

Library of Congress Control Number: 2009910500

Printed in the United States of America
Bloomington, Indiana

This book is printed on acid-free paper.

Author photography by Kristen Stratford

Cover design consultation by Jeff and Audrey Walker

To America's Children and to Those Who Care for Them

TABLE OF CONTENTS

"I am sure the mass of citizens in these United States *mean well*, and I firmly believe they will always *act well* whenever they can obtain a right understanding of matters." - George Washington

FOREWORD

My impetus for writing this book came from two sources. First, I love America. I always have. But for much of my life, I was in a blissful, ignorant slumber regarding politics and governmental issues that was interrupted only intermittently by brief moments of concern. What finally awakened me was the undeniable assault on our freedoms that I started to see within the last year or two. I had become mildly concerned a few years prior, but was unaware of just how significant the encroachments upon our liberties had already been. I did not understand the trends and I did not understand America's founding principles as I should have. As I began to study, I started to realize just how dangerous our current course was.

The second reason for writing this book was the concern my wife and I have for our children. For the past several years we have worked to instill within them a love for America and a reverence for her founding. However, as I began to learn about the threats to our freedoms, I became fearful of what their America would look like. I started sharing what I was learning with them, and I was amazed at how well they understood what I was trying to teach them. I want our kids, and all of America's kids, to grow up in a land of liberty - one that will endure throughout their lives and beyond. For that to happen, they must know America's founding principles and faithfully uphold them.

Combined, these two things sparked within me a desire to create a tool that could be used to teach generations of children, not only what it means to be an American, but also what their duties are in relationship to that privilege. This book is the product of that desire, which now I offer to you and your families.

My fellow Americans,

AMONG ALL THE DIFFERENCES IN our lives, we share at least two grand commonalities. First, we are Americans. Second, we share in the responsibility to keep America great.

We live in the greatest nation the world has ever known. Never has a nation been so willing to help her neighbors, so willing to defend them from tyrants, so willing to rebuild her former enemies, so willing to lift the downtrodden of the earth, or so willing to aid those troubled by natural disasters. America has done all this and so much more and yet she has asked nothing in return. Her military might is unrivaled, her economic power unequaled, her heart great and unconquerable.

Yet, almost unimaginably, America is now in serious danger. And ironically, the greatest danger to her might and sovereignty comes from within her own borders. The very principles she was built on - the ideas that made her great - have been abused, forgotten, and discarded. Without them, she fails. Restore them, and she will never die.

America, "the great experiment" of such humble origins is a gift - not only to her citizens, but to the world. Built upon self-evident truths and the laws of nature, "Nature's God" intended her to be the beacon of freedom that would lift the peoples of the world from the darkness of oppression that has so often plagued His children. But with this gift came a great responsibility. After the Constitution was signed, a woman is reported to have asked Benjamin Franklin, "What have you given us, sir?" His answer: "A Republic, if you can keep it."

My friends, this implies work. Franklin is telling us that we must *maintain* our Republic. This brings me to the second commonality we all share: the responsibility to keep our Republic great. We must keep it from decay. We must patch up its peeling paint and polish its gleaming spires. We do this by remembering America's history, knowing of her founding, understanding her founding principles, and acting accordingly.

Alexis de Tocqueville, commenting on the state of American education in 1831 said, "In New England every citizen receives the elementary notions of human knowledge; he is taught, moreover, the doctrines and the evidences of his religion, the history of his country, and the leading features of its Constitution. In the states of Connecticut and Massachusetts, it is extremely rare to find a man imperfectly acquainted with all these things, and a person wholly ignorant of them is a sort of phenomenon."

Could de Tocqueville make the same observation of our current educational system? I fear not. Were de Tocqueville to visit America today and observe the education of the people, he would undoubtedly describe it as follows: "In America every citizen receives the elementary notions of human knowledge. However, he is, at best, inadequately taught the doctrines and evidences of his religion, the history of his country, and the leading features of its Constitution. It is extremely rare to find an individual moderately acquainted with all these things, and a person wholly knowledgeable of them is a sort of phenomenon."

Just as an uninterested, untrained person cannot perform a successful open heart surgery, so an apathetic, uneducated American public cannot and *will not* maintain our Republic.

So what is to be done? Again we turn to the practical wisdom of Benjamin Franklin.

> "...I think with you, that nothing is of more importance for the public weal, than to form and train up youth in wisdom and virtue. Wise and good men are, in my opinion, the strength of the state; more so than riches or arms....
>
> "I think also, that general virtue is more probably to be expected and obtained from education of youth, than from the exhortations of adult persons; bad habits and vices of the mind being, like diseases of the body, more easily prevented [in youth] than cured [in adults]. I think, moreover, that talents for the education of youth are the gift of God; and that he on whom they are bestowed, whenever a way is opened for the use of them, is as strongly called as if he heard a voice from heaven...."

Herein lies our answer. One of the surest methods to "keep" our Republic, and thus retain our freedoms as outlined in the Constitution, is to instruct our children and grandchildren in the basics of our history, our founding documents, and the principles and sound philosophies that have made America great. This raises the question, "How? How do we accomplish this? Upon which institution do we rely to complete so weighty a task?"

The answer to these questions clear and resounding, "The Family!" The government cannot do it. State-run schools will not do it; at least they are not currently doing so. Perhaps someday in the future the schools will once again catch the vision, but we cannot wait and see; time is of the essence.

Besides, for better or worse, we as parents are our children's first and most effective teachers. What better place for a child to learn to love her country than on her daddy's knee? Who has more impact in instilling within a young boy the virtues our nation was founded upon than his mother? What better place for the first discoveries that "We [*do*] hold these truths to be self-evident" or that "Men *are* endowed by their Creator with certain unalienable rights" than in the home?

What follows are 52 simple discussions concerning our founding principles and the philosophies that are essential for each and every American to know, understand, and cherish. As much as possible, the words come from those who laid the framework for our nation because they were its architects, builders, and masons. It only makes sense, that when seeking to understand the beginnings of our Republic, the most accurate information would come from those who founded it.

For some, this may not be a book to read from cover to cover like a novel, but perhaps a section or two at a time. But however it is read, the hope is that families all across America, regardless of their makeup, will begin to discuss the topics presented herein. Parents, grandparents, children, cousins, aunts, uncles, and friends - around the dinner table, on walks, while biking, in the rocking chair, at the picnic table, around a campfire, on the phone, watching a sunset, at the park, in the living room, tucking a child in at night, or in family prayer. It does not matter how or where the discussion takes place. We must simply gather our children around us and teach. We must instill in them the values that have made America what she is. If we do so, we will keep her and all she stands for. If we don't, we will surely lose her, as well as the freedoms she has given to us and to the world.

When it comes to our Republic, we must all *learn* what we should learn and *do* what we should do. Then, and only then, will we *become* what we must be if we are to keep our Republic: informed, engaged, patriotic Americans.

Let us not lose our Republic. Instead, let us gather our children. Let us instill in them the knowledge, virtues, values, and love of country born of action that, hopefully, were instilled in us. Is short, let us save America, One Child at a Time.

1
WE HOLD THESE TRUTHS
TO BE SELF-EVIDENT

"When in the course of human events, it becomes necessary for one people to dissolve the political bands which have connected them with another, and to assume among the powers of the earth, the separate and equal station to which the laws of nature and of nature's God *entitle* them, a decent respect to the opinions of mankind requires that they should declare the causes which impel them to the separation. – We hold these truths to be self-evident, that all men are created equal, that they are endowed *by their Creator* with certain unalienable rights, that among these are life, liberty and the pursuit of happiness." Declaration of Independence; emphasis added

"If men through fear, fraud or mistake, should in terms renounce and give up any essential natural right, the eternal law of reason and the great end of society, would absolutely vacate such renunciation; the right to freedom being the gift of God Almighty, it is not in the power of Man to alienate this gift, and voluntarily become a slave." John Adams

"The sacred rights of mankind are not to be rummaged for, among old parchments, or musty records. They are written, as with a sun beam, in the whole volume of human nature, by the hand of the divinity itself; and can never be erased or obscured by mortal power." Alexander Hamilton

OUR FOUNDERS WERE MEN OF varied backgrounds. They came from a variety of religions, which some actively practiced, while others preferred a more private type of worship. Others claimed no allegiance to formal religion. Yet on one thing they all agreed: God entitles all mankind to freedom from oppression by other people. Political subservience on any scale is an act against the laws of nature, or, in other words, violates the laws that nature's God has put in place.

The founders also held that all men are created equal. As no two people are born exactly the same, the founders clearly did not mean that all people would (or should) be equal in talent, intelligence, ability to amass wealth, etc. They meant however, that all men were to be treated equally before God and government - that all individuals had the same rights and that those rights would be equally protected unless forfeited by committing a crime against another person or group of people. "Created equal" also means that each individual has the right to make of himself whatever he chooses. Each citizen has the right to succeed or to fail.

Jefferson's original text for the Declaration of Independence included the phrase, "life, liberty, and property." During the ensuing debates, the term "property" was changed to "pursuit of happiness" because the signers did not want slave owners to have perpetual rights on their slaves, which many claimed as property. Therefore, the intent was this: if one, through ingenuity and effort, could obtain property, it was his inalienable right to do so, and government should not interfere. In addition, government should not seek to dictate how the property owner used his property or wealth.

Consequently, ideas such as those given by Theodore Roosevelt in his speech "The New Nationalism" are in direct contradiction to the principles American government was founded upon. Roosevelt stated: "We grudge no man a fortune in civil life if it is honorably obtained and well used. It is not even enough that it should have been gained without doing damage to the community. We should permit it to be gained only so long as the gaining represents benefit to the community." Roosevelt later declared that "every man holds his property subject to the general right of the community to regulate its use to whatever degree the public welfare may require it." Ever since Theodore Roosevelt's presidency, America has been slowly moving toward this manner of thinking, and with every step toward it, we leave behind our inherent rights.

The opening lines of the Declaration of Independence make it clear that because our rights come from God, government is not free to infringe

2

upon them. Government cannot take away what government did not, nor cannot give. According to our founding documents, government cannot dictate how people choose to live their lives or dispose of their property. Each has the unalienable right to determine that for himself.

2

Government Gets Its Power From The People

"That to secure these rights, governments are instituted among men, *deriving* their just powers *from the consent of the governed*." Declaration of Independence; emphasis added

"The fabric of American empire ought to rest on the solid basis of the consent of the people. The streams of national power ought to flow immediately from that pure, original fountain of all legitimate authority." Alexander Hamilton

"The adversaries of the Constitution seem to have lost sight of the people altogether in their reasonings on this subject; and to have viewed these different establishments not only as mutual rivals and enemies, but as uncontrolled by any common superior in their effort to usurp the authorities of each other. These gentlemen must here be reminded of their error. They must be told that the ultimate authority, wherever the derivative may be found, resides in the people alone." James Madison

"Public opinion sets bounds to every government, and is the real sovereign in every free one." James Madison

Our founders understood the need for government, yet at the same time they feared it. George Washington summed up the founders' views on government as follows: "Government is not reason, it is not eloquence, it is force; like fire, a troublesome servant and a fearful master. Never for a moment should it be left to irresponsible action."

4

Fire is not a trusted friend. While it can be a very useful and productive tool, we must employ constant vigilance and never allow it to escape the confines we have placed upon it. Though it is possible to stamp out small breaches of these confines, if allowed to get out of control, fire will take over, consume, and destroy everything in its path, including its former masters - the people who created it. When that happens, the devastation can be immense, and it requires monumental effort to bring it back under control. Government is no different. Government is not our friend. This is a lesson we have forgotten and one that is crucial we remember.

We need to maintain a barrier around government to keep from being burned. To our detriment, we have not heeded Washington's warning that "never for a moment should it be left to irresponsible action." As Americans, we have abandoned our post and left government to grossly irresponsible action. Our national debt is nearly $12,000,000,000,000 and climbing. Continued massive spending on things such as government take-over of business and so-called climate bills that will further cripple our economy, accompanied by legislation from the bench and the greed, corruption, and utter selfishness of elected officials are just a few of the examples too numerous to mention in this setting. Suffice it to say that we have not kept our government under control and the results are proving disastrous.

Because we have left government free to act on its own behalf, many times with popular support, government has taken to itself powers not granted to it under natural law. There are three things we must remember. First, our rights do *not* come from the government. Second, we must remember "that to secure these rights, governments are instituted among men." In other words, government exists to serve its citizens, not the other way around. Third, government derives its just powers from the consent of the governed. Therefore, the only powers government can have are those given to it by the people; the people cannot give government the ability to do what they do not have the right to do themselves. To say it a different way, the powers granted to government are nothing more than the people's natural rights, which are lent to the government; government is to act as a proxy for the people.

For example, Americans have the right to protect themselves and their property. However, most of us are concentrating on making a living and raising our families; duties that render us unable to be in constant protection mode. So, we hire police officers and other law enforcement agents to do much of the protecting for us. In this case, we lend our *inherent right* to protect ourselves to the government.

On the other hand, let's say Chuck has twelve chickens that lay delightful eggs, and Bill has none. Even if I feel it extremely unfair that Bill is denied the exceptional flavor and nutrients of fresh eggs, I do not have the right to go take one (or any other number) of Chuck's chickens and give them to Bill. Thus, since I don't have the right to redistribute Chuck's chicken wealth, government cannot do so either. To restate: government's powers come from me, the citizen, and I cannot lend it powers I do not have myself.

Our children must learn this lesson. We cannot with good conscience subject our posterity to the "fire" of a government that has so drastically overstepped it bounds. We must teach our children the founding principles of our nation lest they slumber in ignorant bliss while their burns become ever more severe.

3
SEPARATION OF CHURCH AND STATE

"History will also afford frequent opportunities of showing
the necessity of a public religion, from its usefulness to
the public; the advantage of a religious character among
private persons, the mischiefs of superstition, etc...."
Benjamin Franklin

OUR CURRENT DEFINITION OF THE separation of church and state is not
what the founders intended. It must be remembered that many, many
of America's early colonists fled here to escape the persecution of an
intolerant, state-sponsored religion. The founders were leery of any type
of tyranny from a powerful government, including religious tyranny, and
accordingly believed that the federal government of the United States
should not sponsor a particular religion.

Though the founders were vehemently opposed to a *state-sponsored*
religion, they never intended that God should be removed from
government. In fact, they believed just the opposite. As we will discuss
later, their writings abound with references to God's hand in establishing
the freedoms enumerated in the Constitution, as well as the need for God's
continuing guidance for their new nation.

The founders also intended that the basic tenets of religion be taught
throughout society, including in the schools, and then practiced among
the general public. This is made indisputably clear by quotes such as this
one from Washington's farewell address:

"Of all the dispositions and habits which lead to political
prosperity, religion and morality are indispensable
supports.... And let us with caution indulge the
supposition that morality can be maintained without
religion.... Reason and experience both forbid us to
expect that national morality can prevail to the exclusion
of religious principle.... It is substantially true that virtue

7

or morality is a necessary spring of popular government....
In vain would that man claim the tribute of patriotism,
who should labor to subvert these great pillars of human
happiness."

Language in the Northwest Ordinance, which Congress passed the
same year the Constitution was written, also underscores our early leaders'
views. Article three reads: "Religion, morality, and knowledge being
necessary to good government and the happiness of mankind, schools and
the means of education shall forever be encouraged."

However, the founders were clear that what was to be taught were
the basic principles of all religion and *not* the specific beliefs of any one
denomination, sect, or group. Benjamin Franklin described them as
follows:

> "Here is my creed: I believe in one God, the Creator of
> the universe. That he governs it by his providence. That
> he ought to be worshipped. That the most acceptable
> service we render to him is in doing good to his other
> children. That the soul of man is immortal, and will be
> treated with justice in another life respecting its conduct
> in this. These I take to be the fundamental points in all
> sound religion."

These were the principles the founding fathers believed and wanted
taught throughout America, including in the schools. When writing about
his visit to America in 1831, Alexis de Tocqueville noted that the spirit of
religion and the spirit of freedom were "intimately united," and that while
"religion in America takes no direct part in the government of society,...
it must be regarded as the first of their political institutions." He also
commented that "there is no country in the world where the Christian
religion retains a greater influence over the souls of men than in America."
De Tocqueville further observed that:

> "I sought for the greatness and genius of America in her
> commodious harbors and her ample rivers, and it was
> not there; in her fertile fields and boundless prairies, and
> it was not there; in her rich mines and her vast world
> commerce, and it was not there. Not until I went to the
> churches of America and heard her pulpits aflame with
> righteousness did I understand the secret of her genius

and power. America is great because she is good, and if America ever ceases to be good, America will cease to be great."

W. Cleon Skousen, in his book *The 5000 Year Leap*, summed up the original intent of the idea that America needed a separation of church and state: "There was separation of church and state but not a separation of state and religion." Our Republic cannot thrive in the absence of religion.

4
Only A Virtuous People Are Capable Of Freedom

"Our Constitution was made only for a moral and religious people. It is wholly inadequate to the government of any other." John Adams

"It is substantially true that virtue or morality is a necessary spring of popular government." George Washington

"I thank God that I have lived to see my country independent and free. She may long enjoy her independence and freedom if she will. It depends on her virtue." Samuel Adams

"The sum of all is, if we would most truly enjoy the gift of Heaven, let us become a virtuous people; then shall we both deserve and enjoy it. While, on the other hand, if we are universally vicious and debauched in our manners, though the form of our Constitution carries the face of the most exalted freedom, we shall in reality be the most abject slaves." Samuel Adams

"The only foundation of a free Constitution, is pure virtue...." John Adams

"Is there no virtue among us? If there be not, we are in a wretched situation. No theoretical checks, no form of government, can render us secure. To suppose that any form of government will secure liberty or happiness without any virtue in the people, is a chimerical [imaginary] idea." James Madison

"Only a virtuous people are capable of freedom. As nations become corrupt and vicious, they have more need of masters." Benjamin Franklin

AMERICA'S GOVERNING DOCUMENT BEGINS WITH the words, "We the People of the United States." We are a government "of the people, by the people, and for the people"; we are to govern *ourselves*. Only a just and a virtuous people are capable of doing so. A just and virtuous people will prosper under the freedoms prescribed in the Constitution simply because they are good. They will enact just laws and abide by them. They will work hard to be as self-sufficient as possible, they will look after each other, and they will be at peace with their neighbors. A corrupt and immoral people will not. An immoral people will seek for power. They will lie, cheat, steal, bribe, and enact unjust laws. In short, they will trample and destroy the very freedoms and self-government that made them great.

5
America The Beautiful

Oh, beautiful for spacious skies,
For amber waves of grain,
For purple mountain majesties
Above the fruited plain!
America! America!
God shed his grace on thee,
And crown thy good with brotherhood
From sea to shining sea.

Oh, beautiful for pilgrim feet,
Whose stern, impassioned stress
A thoroughfare of freedom beat
Across the wilderness!
America! America!
God mend thine every flaw,
Confirm thy soul in self-control,
Thy liberty in law.

Oh, beautiful for heroes proved
In liberating strife,
Who more than self their country loved,
And mercy more than life!
America! America!
May God thy gold refine,
Till all success be nobleness,
And every gain divine.

Oh, beautiful for patriot dream
That sees beyond the years
Thine alabaster cities gleam,

Undimmed by human tears!
America! America!
God shed his grace on thee,
And crown thy good with brotherhood
From sea to shining sea.

THIS HYMN OF AMERICAN VIRTUES, written by Katherine Lee Bates, beautifully portrays many of the notions that have made America what it is. A careful reading of it brings with it a profound understanding of America's goodness and what she was intended to be. That understanding, in turn, generates feelings of gratitude for what we enjoy in this nation, and a yearning to keep her great wells up within us.

Brotherhood is one of America's crowning virtues. We are an amalgamation of different nations unlike the world has ever seen. The merging of differences that have destroyed other civilizations is one of America's greatest strengths. Will it remain so? We are now becoming a people of hyphens - a people divided by race, creed, and political philosophy. There is significant beauty in the variety of people within America's borders. But let us remember that we are Americans first and foremost; united in the cause of freedom.

The song *America the Beautiful* answers the question "to whom do we seek to mend our flaws?" Are we petitioning that Source? Have we made the political matters that perplex our nation a matter of prayer? Do we seek Divine guidance on the issues that divide us? Do we appeal to Providence for wisdom in our personal lives? Do we ask the great Peacemaker for unity in our families, communities, and nation?

America is held firm through the self-control of her people and by adherence to law. How much self-control do we, as citizens, exercise? Is it sufficient? Are there those who, because of power, connections, or money, flout our laws?

Do we have heroes today who have been *proven* through liberating strife or through other means? Do we even have heroes? Do we love country more than self, or have we fallen prey to the "me first" attitude that is so prevalent today? Do we love mercy or do we seek revenge and retribution for supposed wrongs? Do we accept challenges as refining? Do we resolutely face and conquer them, thus allowing our successes to be noble and our gains divine? Or do we whimper and seek the easy way out, thereby fostering weakness?

Are we patriots who see beyond the years? Do we have the vision of America - what she is, and what she can be? Do we strive to realize that vision? Or do we sell ourselves, our children, and our country short by focusing on our own wants?

America! America!
God shed his grace on thee,
And crown thy good with brotherhood
From sea to shining sea.

Do we feel this plea deep within our hearts? Are we working to make it a reality?

6
Our Founders Believed Their Work Was Inspired Of God

"[The adoption of the Constitution] will demonstrate as visibly the finger of Providence as any possible event in the course of human affairs can ever designate it." George Washington

"Doctor Rush then proceeded to consider the origin of the proposed [Constitution], and fairly deduced it [was] from heaven, asserting that he as much believed the hand of God was employed in this work as that God had divided the Red Sea to give passage to the children of Israel, or had fulminated the Ten Commandments from Mount Sinai." Benjamin Rush

"The real wonder is that so many difficulties should have been surmounted, and surmounted with a unanimity almost as unprecedented as it must have been unexpected. It is impossible for any man of candor to reflect on this circumstance without partaking of the astonishment. It is impossible for the man of pious reflection not to perceive in it a finger of that Almighty hand which has been so frequently and signally extended to our relief in the critical stages of the revolution." James Madison

"I have so much faith in the general government of the world by Providence that I can hardly conceive a transaction of such momentous importance [as the framing of the Constitution]…should be suffered to pass without being in some degree influenced, guided, and governed by that omnipotent, omnipresent, and beneficent Ruler in whom all inferior spirits live and move and have their being." Benjamin Franklin

"It appears to me...little short of a miracle that the delegates from so many different states (which states... are also different from each other in their manners, circumstances, and prejudices) should unite in forming a system of national government so little liable to well-founded objections." George Washington

A MIRACLE INDEED! IF ONE truly studies the early history of America, its revolution and founding, it must be acceded that this nation is the product of more than the efforts of an unlikely group of rag-tag soldiers and a handful of visionary, dedicated men. If, as our founders believed, nature's God played a hand in the foundation of our Republic, should we not defend it as well? If, as our founders believed, "the finger of Providence" pointed the way to the creation and adoption of the Constitution, shall we not teach, live by, and defend the principles of the Constitution? There is only one rational answer to these questions, and that answer is yes.

7
THE FOUNDING FATHERS DID NOT SEEK FOR PERSONAL GAIN

WHAT DID THE DRAFTERS AND signers of the Declaration of Independence gain for their efforts? Perhaps a more appropriate question would be, what did the drafters and signers of the Declaration of Independence *give*? Quite literally, they gave exactly what they pledged to give: their lives, their liberty, and their sacred honor. They knew that by signing that document they were committing an act of treason against the most powerful empire in the world. Benjamin Franklin commented, "Indeed we must all hang together, otherwise we shall most assuredly all hang separately." The signers knew there would be no financial reward, no comfy pensions, no retirement with benefits. They knew they would be hunted mercilessly and their families put in peril.

In a speech entitled The Americans Who Risked Everything, Rush. H. Limbaugh, Jr. summed their sacrifices up as follows:

> "Of those 56 who signed the Declaration of Independence, nine died of wounds or hardships during the war. Five were captured and imprisoned, in each case with brutal treatment. Several lost wives, sons or entire families. One lost his 13 children. Two wives were brutally treated. All were at one time or another the victims of manhunts and driven from their homes. Twelve signers had their homes completely burned. Seventeen lost everything they owned. Yet not one defected or went back on his pledged word. Their honor...is still intact.
>
> "And, finally, there is the New Jersey signer, Abraham Clark. He gave two sons to the officer corps in the Revolutionary Army. They were captured and sent to that infamous British prison hulk afloat in New York Harbor known as the hell ship Jersey, where 11,000 American captives were to die. The younger Clarks were treated

with a special brutality because of their father. One was put in solitary and given no food. With the end almost in sight, with the war almost won, no one could have blamed Abraham Clark for acceding to the British request when they offered him his sons' lives if he would recant and come out for the King and Parliament. The utter despair in this man's heart, the anguish in his very soul, must reach out to each one of us down through 200 years with his answer: 'No.'"

Who can say that these men and their families were not utterly and selflessly committed to their beloved new nation? And what of the other nameless thousands who made supreme sacrifices for the cause of America? Are we and our families worthy of the commitment and sacrifice they made on our behalf?

Regarding those who crafted the Constitution, James Madison said:

"Whatever may be the judgment pronounced on the competency of the architects of the Constitution, or whatever may be the destiny of the edifice prepared by them, I feel it a duty to express my profound and solemn conviction…that there never was an assembly of men charged with a great and arduous trust who were more pure in their motives, or more exclusively or anxiously devoted to the object committed to them, than were the members of the Federal Convention of 1787 to the object of devising and proposing a constitutional system which should…best secure the permanent liberty and happiness of their country."

Consider today's politicians, those who have been entrusted by us to defend and uphold the supreme law of our land. Are they "pure in their motives?" Are they "anxiously devoted to the object" of keeping America free, strong, and independent? Are we? Have our politicians, like the signers of the Declaration really pledged their lives, their liberty, and their sacred honor? Have we? If the answers to any of these questions are, as I fear, no, then perhaps it is time to make some changes. Perhaps it is time to question our leaders. Perhaps it is time to question ourselves. And perhaps it is time to teach our children to do the same.

8
GRATITUDE

"That I may be grateful to my benefactors…Help me, O Father! … And, forasmuch as ingratitude is one of the most odious vices, let me not be unmindful gratefully to acknowledge the favors I receive from Heaven." Benjamin Franklin

"Nothing is a greater stranger to my breast, or a sin that my soul [more abhors], than that black and detestable one, ingratitude." George Washington

"Ingratitude…I hope will never constitute a part of my character, nor find a place in my bosom." George Washington

"These are the times that try men's souls. The summer soldier and the sunshine patriot will, in this crisis, shrink from the service of his country; but he that stands it now, deserves the love and thanks of man and woman." Thomas Paine

WE ARE AMONG THE MEN and women spoken of by Thomas Paine. We are the direct beneficiaries of the sacrifices of the revolutionary Americans. We are also the beneficiaries of the sacrifices that so many other selfless Americans have made throughout the ensuing years, that we may enjoy unmatched prosperity and liberty. They do indeed deserve our love and gratitude. Are we grateful? Are we *sufficiently* grateful?

Gratitude is one of the hallmarks of polite, civil society, the kind of society that is necessary for our Republic to thrive. Therefore, we should consistently express it. It is remarkable how a sincere thank-you or an appreciative compliment can lift a person's mood. Have we thanked the mailman, a teacher, a co-worker, or a stranger on the street that is kind? Have we expressed thanks to our spouse or children, or to our brothers or sisters or parents? Are we found on our knees thanking God for the miracle that is America and for the absolute privilege to live within her borders? Do we thank our political leaders, city council, school board members, and others when they make correct decisions or serve honorably?

Expressions of appreciation or simple words of gratitude for a kind act or a job well done will usually breed more of the same. Hence, the more we say thanks, the more reasons we will have to continue saying it.

9
FREEDOM MUST BE MAINTAINED
IF IT IS TO BE PRESERVED

"No compact among men…can be pronounced everlasting and inviolable, and if I may so express myself, that no Wall of words, that no mound of parchment can be so formed as to stand against the sweeping torrent of boundless ambition on the one side, aided by the sapping current of corrupted morals on the other." George Washington

"There are more instances of the abridgement of the freedom of the people by gradual and silent encroachments of those in power than by violent and sudden usurpations." James Madison

"It remains with the people themselves to preserve and promote the great advantages of their political and natural situation…." George Washington

"Every man who loves peace, every man who loves his country, every man who loves liberty ought to have it ever before his eyes that he may cherish in his heart a due attachment to the Union of America and be able to set a due value on the means of preserving it." James Madison

"Those who expect to reap the blessings of freedom, must, like men, undergo the fatigues of supporting it." Thomas Paine

"What we obtain too cheap, we esteem too lightly: it is dearness only that gives everything its value." Thomas Paine

"...a Constitution of Government once changed from Freedom, can never be restored. Liberty, once lost, is lost forever." John Adams

WE MUST BEWARE. WE MUST be vigilant. For at least the last one hundred years, our freedoms have been slipping away - sometimes subtly, sometimes glaringly, and often under the "justification" born of emergency. A few examples include Theodore Roosevelt's attacks on private property and Woodrow Wilson arresting or jailing dissidents. Wilson also undermined civil liberties, such as with his attacks on the free press, and he used massive propaganda to promote his agenda. FDR's New Deal and the so-called Fairness Doctrine are other examples.

More recent examples of government reducing individual liberties include laws requiring the use of seat belts and bike helmets. It may be a good idea to wear seat belts and bike helmets but should government *mandate* that they be worn? Some may argue that these are just little things and that the government just has our best interests in mind. Perhaps, but if we are silent on the small things that "are good ideas anyway," where will it end?

Will it end with government taking over banks and corporations? Will it end with government capping the salaries of executives? Maybe it will be over when Congress passes a law that allows it to exorbitantly tax certain individuals because it disagrees with the bonuses they've received. Perhaps it will be sufficient encroachment on individual liberty if government could reach into our homes and regulate our thermostats or monitor each person's "carbon footprint". Maybe, but then again, maybe not. It may well be that when it comes to taking our freedoms, the government is just warming up.

De Tocqueville's warning still rings true today: "It must not be forgotten that it is especially dangerous to enslave men in the minor details of life. For my own part, I should be inclined to think freedom less necessary in great things than in little ones."

We must resist governmental encroachment of individual liberty on any level, even if we think giving up liberty may make us "safer." Benjamin Franklin said that "they who can give up essential liberty to obtain a little temporary safety deserve neither liberty nor safety."

Where would we be if our founders had been content with having less liberty so they could play it safe? Samuel Adams had strong words for those who sit idly by while government seeks to become their master. He said that those who favor the "tranquility of servitude" better be ready to "crouch down and lick the hands which feed you....May your chains sit lightly upon you, and may posterity forget that you were our countrymen!" (Beck 2009)

Will we rise up and demand government live within its bounds? Will we assert our inalienable rights? Or will we be content to rattle our chains and lick government's benevolent hand? The choice is ours; but as we make it, we should keep in mind the advice of the man referred to as the father of our nation, who considered it "a crime" to remain silent on issues relating to our freedoms:

> "It should be the highest ambition of every American to extend his views beyond himself, and to bear in mind that his conduct will not only affect himself, his country, and his immediate posterity; but that its influence may be co-extensive with the world, and stamp political happiness or misery on ages yet unborn." George Washington

10
AMERICAN CITIZENS MUST MINGLE
AND DISCUSS THESE ISSUES

WHERE WOULD AMERICA BE WITHOUT the taverns and Masonic lodges of the eighteenth century? Would the Constitution have been ratified without discussion of the Federalist Papers? Where would our country be if half the people had not been reading (or had read to them) and discussing Thomas Paine's *Common Sense*? The first Americans were not all of one mind. They had *strongly* differing opinions. Some were Tories who were loyal to the British crown. Others were all for separation from England. There were also those who weren't sure what they wanted or what, if anything, should be done. They were all worried about English reprisals. They wondered "What will become of our homes, our families, our children?" Many questioned whether the infringements upon their rights as Englishmen, the taxation, or being forced to board English troops was sufficient cause for doing something.

Aside from time and circumstance, those early Americans were just like us. We have the same questions and concerns, and our opinions often differ from those of our neighbors. So what was it that brought Colonial Americans together? What caused the galvanization sufficient to rally them to declare their independence, endure untold hardship, and overcome all odds as a group of relatively untrained farmers took on and defeated the greatest military power in the world?

The answer, in part, is because they met. They talked, they argued, and they conversed over the pertinent ideas and events of the day. They shared their own views and listened to those of others. I believe it was this phenomenon, as much as any other, that brought a people, a new nation, together. Our forbearers surely did not agree on all of the details, but they were sufficiently united in the cause of American freedom to get the job done.

Today, we are *capable* of doing the same, but are we *willing*? It's time to get out of our comfort zones and mingle with our neighbors. We have break rooms at work. There are layovers in airports, not to mention the long flights themselves that we spend shoulder to shoulder with fellow passengers - fellow Americans - who have the same concerns we do. There are meeting halls galore in this nation. There are backyards and living rooms in every community. The internet and blogs can be useful tools for sharing ideas and organizing, but nothing will ever replace the need for face-to-face discussion. Nothing short of close, personal interaction will suffice for what we need to accomplish.

We will not agree on all the particulars of government, and we should not expect or wait for that moment of perfect unanimity; it will never happen. Besides, many of our differences in opinion are immaterial to the matter at hand, because for all our differences in circumstance and opinion, we are very much the same. We love our country. We want a safe place to raise our children. We are concerned about the national debt and other disturbing trends within government and society in general. We want something done; we just differ in the details of what should be done or how to do it.

It does not matter that we don't know all the answers. What matters is that we begin to meet with our families and neighbors. It is time to talk. It is time to learn from others' views. It is time to discuss the issues of today. It is time to discuss the principles our nation was founded upon. It is time to find common ground. It is time to unite once more. It is time to become involved Americans. It is time.

11

An Educated Electorate

"In proportion as the structure of a government gives force to public opinion, it is essential that public opinion should be enlightened." George Washington

"Enlightened statesmen will not always be at the helm." James Madison

"Wisdom and knowledge, as well as virtue, diffused generally among the body of the people, [are] necessary for the preservation of their rights and liberties...." John Adams

"The fundamental source of all your errors, sophisms and false reasonings is a total ignorance of the natural rights of mankind. Were you once to become acquainted with these, you could never entertain a thought, that all men are not, by nature, entitled to a parity of privileges. You would be convinced, that natural liberty is a gift of the beneficent Creator to the whole human race, and that civil liberty is founded in that; and cannot be wrested from any people, without the most manifest violation of justice." Alexander Hamilton

"No other sure foundation can be devised for the preservation of freedom and happiness.... Preach...a crusade against ignorance; establish and improve the law for educating the common people. Let our countrymen know that *the people alone* can protect us against these evils [of misgovernment]." Thomas Jefferson; emphasis added

"If a nation expects to be ignorant and free, in a state of civilization, it expects what never was and never will be."
Thomas Jefferson

Referring to Thomas Jefferson, James Madison wrote: "He was certainly one of the most learned men of the age. It may be said of him as has been said of others that he was a 'walking library,' and what can be said of but few such prodigies, that the Genius of Philosophy ever walked hand in hand with him."

"Children should be educated and instructed in the principles of freedom." John Adams

THOSE WHO ESTABLISHED THE FREEDOMS and government of the United States of America were very well read; they were students of history, government, philosophy, science, and many other disciplines. They never could have done what they did otherwise! The same applies for us today. As Jefferson said, we cannot be ignorant and expect to be free. That being so, it is little wonder that our freedoms are slipping through our fingers at an ever-increasing pace. We have become ignorant of our past and of the science of government. True, we have mastered technologies early Americans never dreamed of. Yes, we go to elementary and high school. Sure, we graduate from colleges and graduate schools. And we have, without a doubt, achieved the highest standard of living ever known to the world. Yet we do not know our own history and form of government. We talk of patriotism and sacrifice on a couple of holidays, but what do we know of them? Can we look at a law passed by Congress or an action taken by the President or the Supreme Court and determine if it was constitutional or not?

The sad truth is that the average American knows very little to nothing about the turmoil and heartache that so many have endured for our sake and the sake of our freedoms. We know almost nothing about the writings and political philosophies of those who laid the foundation of the greatest nation on earth, let alone the writings of those who influenced them: Cicero, Blackstone, Burke, Locke, Sidney, Adam Smith. Do we even know who these men were?

What do we know of the American Revolution? When is the last time, if ever, that we read the Constitution, the Declaration of Independence, or the Articles of Confederation? In fact, what are the Articles of Confederation, and for that matter, what is a republican form of government? The bigger question may be, why didn't we learn these things in school? Why weren't they taught to us every year starting in kindergarten?

A clue to the answer is given to us by President Woodrow Wilson. Wilson went to great lengths to sway public opinion to favor his agenda. And just in case that didn't work, he had thousands of people spied on, hassled, or thrown in jail for private opinions that differed from his. He knew what he wanted and he was out to get it. He was also shrewd enough to know that if he could influence the youth, he'd have an easier time of it. While still the president of Princeton, he said, "Our problem is not merely to help the students to adjust themselves to world life…[but] to make them as unlike their fathers as we can" (Goldberg 2007). To him, education was a chance to indoctrinate. Unfortunately, that sentiment did not die with him. One merely has to observe to discover that the ideas of Wilson and his fellow progressives on education still infest all levels of education in our country.

We see our kids come home with propaganda on various topics, with environmental issues seeming to take center stage. In some schools, our children have even been subjected to compelling video propaganda, indicating that they should make a pledge to become a "servant" of our current President. In addition, President Obama's recent incursion into the nationwide public school system to speak to all of our children, calls to mind the early progressive thought on influencing children through the educational system.

Do we politely resist or question? It is our duty as American citizens, and as parents, to do so. We must resist, question, or if need be, refuse to participate in any line of thought or in any activity that is not in the best interest of our children or our country. At the same time, we need to start insisting that the essentials of American history and government be taught once again. Some of the teachers and administrators will not like it. Some may get angry. So what? Our concern is not what they think; our concern as Americans is what is best for our nation and our families. We stay firm, but polite.

On the other hand, there will be those teachers and administrators - and who knows, maybe even a government official or two - who will be delighted in and applaud our efforts. With time and patience, our numbers will swell, and needed changes will then be effected. However, in the meantime and even after, we must continue to educate ourselves and our children. If we succeed today in reaching one child at a time through education and example, we save a generation. That generation will in turn, save the next.

Only an enlightened and educated electorate will have the ability to understand and force change when our elected statesmen are not, as Madison predicted, "enlightened" themselves.

Jefferson said, "I think it is Montaigne who has said that ignorance is the softest pillow on which a man can rest his head. I am sure it is true as to everything political, and shall endeavor to estrange myself to everything of that character."

If we will adopt Jefferson's attitude on ignorance, we will become the electorate our nation so desperately needs.

12
BACK TO BASICS

The world we live in; so complex,
     so rushed, and fast paced too.
We hurry here we hurry there,
     "important" things to do.
So busy are we, we forget,
     the way things used to be,
Like riding bikes, or playing catch,
     or sitting in a tree.
"On to fame and fortune!"
     the chant rings loud and clear,
So loud in fact that we don't hear
     that quiet, softly whispered voice
     that tells us why we're here.
"Forget about the fancy car"
     the voice so softly pleads,
"Instead go spend sometime at home
     or care for others needs."
What happened to the better way
     that people used to live?
The life of love and sharing
     and happy just to give.
A self-rewarding, happy life
     comes not from coin or dollar,
It doesn't come to those on top
     nor to those standing taller.
A fulfilling and contented life comes on quiet wings,
     like hearing softly whispering pines
     or the song the robin sings.
Thank God for trickling little streams
     and meadows filled with flowers,

For snowflakes, puppies, ducks, and dreams,
    and all those happy little things
    that make for pleasant hours.
Our Creator gave us all these gifts
    and countless other kinds,
Let's show him we are thankful
    by enjoying all we find.
The world we live in, full of cares,
    presses onward fast and cold,
And sadly many people find
    they've died before they're old.
So learn to like a new green leaf
    and all mankind to love,
And you will find that inner peace
    that comes from heav'n above.

ALL OF US ARE BUSY. Every American of every generation has faced challenges and setbacks, and we always will. Trouble and difficulty are just part of our existence as human beings. However, we can lessen their effects by focusing on what really matters: our God, our country, our spouses, our children, our friends, neighbors, and communities. If we center our passions, energies, and efforts on what matters most, including our freedoms and government, we will never be found wanting.

13
Remember

"Let them now begin to read...the best histories of our own nation and colonies. Let emulation be excited.... This will make them read with attention, and imprint the history well in their memories." Benjamin Franklin

It has been said that if a nation does not remember the past, it is destined to repeat it.

Do we remember? Do we remember the principles this nation was founded upon? Do we constantly call to mind the faith, dedication, and endurance of the thousands of Americans who fought, bled, toiled, and gave their lives, fortunes, and sacred honor to found the United States of America? Do we remember the wars our country has fought and is currently fighting? Do we remember those who died? Do we remember why they died? Do we remember the nobility of America? Do we remember the successes of former generations and their leaders? Do we remember their mistakes and failures? Do we keep in mind our own success and failures? Do we remember the roots of the current challenges we face in America? Do we remember?

What have we learned from what we remember? It is not enough to not forget. The word *remember* is a verb; it implies action, it is not passive. It takes work and a concerted effort to do so.

We must remember. And we must act accordingly.

14
THE PURPOSE OF THE CONSTITUION

THE INTENT OF THE CONSTITUTION is set forward in its opening paragraph:

> "**We the People** of the United States, in Order to form a more perfect Union, establish Justice, insure domestic Tranquility, provide for the common defense, promote the general Welfare, and secure the Blessings of Liberty to ourselves and our Posterity, do ordain and establish this Constitution for the United States of America."

Not a bad set of goals, if you think about them. In actuality, the purposes of our Constitution are noble and lofty, not to mention very unusual for the governments of the age. What's more, those purposes have been beautifully delivered.

Our Constitution was meant to stand as an example to the world for ages to come, and it will do so as long as we do not fail it. It would not be until courts, congressmen, presidents, those who aspire for power and influence, and a misguided citizenry started to abuse, distort, or ignore the Constitution that it would face any real threat. Sadly however, the assault began decades ago. It remains to us, the Americans of today, to intervene, to stem the attack, and to reverse course.

If we are among those who like the ideas of justice, tranquility, common defense, or the blessings of liberty, than let us stand for them. Let us teach them to our children and discuss them with our neighbors and associates. Let us demand that our elected leaders uphold our founding document, or let us remove them from their station and elect other, more noble-minded individuals for office.

Our Constitution has not failed us, we have failed it. The Constitution has stood the test of time; we as a people have not. Let us rectify our actions and become a constitutional people once again. After all, if the current direction of our government is indicative of the alternative, we have a great deal to lose. John Adams described the type of society that would exist under a constitution such as ours:

> "A constitution founded on these principles introduces knowledge among the people, and inspires them with a conscious dignity becoming freemen; a general emulation takes place, which causes good humor, sociability, good manners, and good morals to be general. That elevation of sentiment inspired by such a government, makes the common people brave and enterprising. That ambition which is inspired by it makes them sober, industrious, and frugal."

If this is the type of society we wish for ourselves and our children, we must espouse, uphold, and defend the depository of the principles that can deliver it. In our case, that depository is the Constitution of the United States of America.

15
ELECT WISE AND VIRTUOUS LEADERS

"I love to see honest and honorable men at the helm, men who will not bend their politics to their purses, nor pursue measures by which they may profit, and then profit by their measures." Thomas Jefferson

"As good government is an empire of laws, how shall your laws be made? In a large society, inhabiting an extensive country, it is impossible that the whole should assemble to make laws. The first necessary step, then, is to depute power from the many to a few of the most wise and good." John Adams

"I Pray Heaven to Bestow The Best of Blessing on THIS HOUSE, and on ALL that shall hereafter Inhabit it. May none but Honest and Wise Men ever rule under This Roof!" John Adams; while President of the United States

WHY SHOULD WE SEEK OUT and elect "the most wise and good" among us as governmental leaders? This is obviously a rhetorical question, especially if one takes a moment to look at the rabble that occupy many of the governmental seats at all levels, from local to national, as well as the laws, regulations, etc., that come from them.

We cannot place worms on an apple tree and rationally expect picture-perfect, tasty apples. We cannot spread infectious bacteria through our homes and expect to remain healthy. To do so would defy common sense, and yet we elect, reelect, and then reelect again corrupt, selfish, greedy people to office. We bemoan the state of affairs in the country and wonder why everything is so messed up and getting worse. WE DEMAND CHANGE ...and then we elect more of the same. No wonder we're sick and our apples breed worms.

There is a better way. We can seek out and encourage the most wise and good among us to run for office, and we can help them get there. George Washington was one of those men. He did not want to be president. He would much rather have been "at Mount Vernon with a friend or two about [him], than to be attended at the Seat of Government by the Officers of State and the Representatives of every Power in Europe." However, he "was summoned by [his] country, whose voice [he could] never hear but with veneration and love." Those who are encouraged to run should seriously consider it and, if possible, should do so. Benjamin Franklin's attitude toward public office is worthy of consideration: "I shall never *ask*, never *refuse*, nor ever *resign* an office."

Of course, our current political system with its two primary parties, the cost of campaigns, and so forth, may make running for office and winning nearly impossible, but that should not stop us from trying to get virtuous people elected. We should seek out those who view public office in the same way that Jefferson did, namely, that "public employment contributes neither to advantage nor happiness. It is but honorable exile from one's family and affairs."

As Americans, we can and must assert our desire for wise and virtuous leaders in government. Over time, as our cities and states start hearing from good, constitutionally grounded, decent individuals who are running for office because they were asked to and not because they are seeking power, the message will get out, and the votes will surely come.

The electoral process is one of the greatest protections our founders gave us. It is like a great shield that we can call upon to deflect governmental assaults upon our liberties. It is time we polish it up and bring it to our defense once more. The results will be well worth the effort.

16
LOYALTY

"That I may be loyal to my Prince, and faithful to my country, careful for its good, valiant in its defense, and obedient to its laws, abhorring treason as much as tyranny – Help me, O Father!" Benjamin Franklin

"There is a certain enthusiasm in liberty, that makes human nature rise above itself, in acts of bravery and heroism." Alexander Hamilton

WE MUST, WITHOUT QUESTION, BE true to our Constitution and to the nation established by it, for these are what ensure us our freedoms and liberty. I believe most Americans agree that we owe the country and the Constitution our deepest loyalty and commitment. That being said, it is possible we have placed a misguided (though well intentioned) sense of loyalty in our government, even as it has amassed unconstitutional powers at the expense of our inalienable rights and liberties. We do not owe our allegiance to ill-meaning or ignorant politicians, or to the form of government they have created; we owe our allegiance to our Republic as put in place by the Constitution.

Colonial Americans loved their country, which was England. They had no desire to break from her. With loyal intent, they sought to right wrongs while they asserted their rights as English citizens. They were loyal subjects of the king, and they wanted to be treated and recognized as such. They simply did not want the rights and privileges afforded them as Englishmen to be taken away from them.

Today in America we find ourselves in the same predicament. The rights and privileges due us as American citizens, including our rightful place at the head of government, are being taken from us. A sense of loyalty to the officials and policies of government responsible for this encroachment is actually disloyalty to our nation, disloyalty to our fellow Americans, and disloyalty to our founding documents.

Let us once again be loyal to our country. We do this by speaking out, resisting unconstitutional and unwise change, educating ourselves and the rising generation, and working to bring government back within the bounds established by our wise, unselfish founders.

We must also be loyal to that God who, through His guiding providence, gave us our inalienable rights and freedoms in the first place.

Let us be up and at it. Let us be truly loyal to this great nation.

17
FEDERAL POWER IS LIMITED

"The enumeration in the Constitution, of certain rights, shall not be construed to deny or disparage others retained by the people." The Ninth Amendment

"The powers not delegated to the United States by the Constitution, nor prohibited by it to the States, are reserved to the States respectively, or to the people." The Tenth Amendment

"I consider the foundation of the Constitution as laid on this ground: 'that all powers not delegated to the United States by the Constitution, nor prohibited by it to the States, are reserved to the States or to the people.'... To take a *single step* beyond the boundaries thus specifically drawn around the powers of Congress is to take possession of a boundless field of power, no longer susceptible of any definition." Thomas Jefferson; emphasis added

"The proposed Constitution, so far from implying an abolition of the State governments, makes them constituent parts of the national sovereignty, by allowing them a direct representation in the Senate, and leaves in their possession certain exclusive and very important portions of sovereign power. This fully corresponds, in every rational import of the terms, with the idea of a federal government." Alexander Hamilton

THE FIRST AMERICAN GOVERNMENT WAS created by the Articles of Confederation, not the Constitution. Needing some sort of central government after declaring independence from Great Britain, the Articles of Confederation were penned in 1777 but not ratified until 1781. Because the states feared a strong central power, the Articles put into place a weak central government. It was so weak that, among other things, it could not raise a standing army, which made war with the powerful British even more difficult.

Both during and after the Revolutionary War, it became apparent that the Articles were far too weak to hold the states together with any semblance of cohesiveness, so it was undertaken to draft a different form of governance - one with a stronger central government. It must be remembered that the early Americans were very distrustful of any strong, centralized form of government. And who can blame them. After what they had been through with England, the states wanted to maintain as much of their sovereignty as they could; they did not want their hard-earned freedoms given over to another despot.

As such, the product of this second round of government creation, the Constitution, lined out specifically what powers the federal government was to have. Its drafters were attempting to create a central government with sufficient power to hold the union intact while at the same time setting the bounds needed to ensure that state powers and individual rights would not be violated. Even so, there were still some states that were leery of the proposed Constitution. Thus, in an attempt to alleviate their misgivings, the Bill of Rights was added to help solidify state and individual rights.

The tenth amendment is very clear: whatever power neither specifically given to the federal government in the Constitution, nor specifically prohibited to the states belongs to the states and the citizens who reside in them. Thus, the federal government, while being granted sufficient power to do its work, was limited by boundaries it could not cross. The trouble is, that over time, the federal government has not only crossed these boundaries, but has in some cases annihilated them.

The federal government, in part, was empowered to declare war, organize and arm a militia, regulate commerce with foreign nations, coin money, fix the standard of weights and measures, and establish post offices. The Constitution does not give the federal government the power to be involved in education or welfare, to establish a central bank, to dictate how a state conducts business within the state, or to set aside federal conservation lands. These are just a few examples of federal theft of state sovereignty.

If the powers not specifically enumerated for the federal government are reserved for the states, how is it that we have the federal government dictating test scores? How did we get the Federal Reserve? Why do we have federal lands within the states? What about Social Security, Medicare, Medicaid, and other federally funded welfare programs? Part of the problem lies with corrupt and cowardly courts, and part of it lies with powerful presidents and other politicians who used the bully pulpit and other means to ram their unconstitutional agendas through. Another large part of the problem lies with us - we who stood by and let it happen. After all, who can argue with conservation, right? And who doesn't want government-funded retirement? Wouldn't that make life easier?

Can we ever completely force the federal government back into its original sphere? I don't know. Much of the answer may lie with the question of how much we as a people are once again willing to be responsible for in our own lives. Federal and state handouts are very enticing to many.

To round out this discussion, we must also consider the more recent encroachments of federal power into forbidden arenas: Troubled Asset Relief Program (TARP) monies, stimulus packages, government takeover of banks and other businesses, climate change legislation and federal involvement in other environmental issues, and so-called national health care bills.

We have arrived at the place Alexander Hamilton warned of when he said "If the federal government should overpass the just bounds of its authority and make a tyrannical use of its powers, the people, whose creature it is, must appeal to the standard they have formed, and take such measures to redress the injury done to the Constitution as the exigency may suggest and prudence justify."

We must draw the line. We must defend the Constitution. We cannot let the federal government steal any more power. The Constitution is the supreme law of the land. We should not allow those who swore to uphold it to violate it. No one is, or should be, above the law.

18
TEACH OUR CHILDREN VIRTUE AND MORALITY

"When we are planning for posterity, we ought to remember that virtue is not hereditary." Thomas Paine

"You cannot be more pleased in talking about your children, your methods of instructing them, and the progress they make, than I am in hearing it, and in finding that, instead of following the idle amusements which both your fortune and the custom of the age might have led you into, your delight and your duty go together by employing your time in the education of your offspring. *This is following nature and reason, instead of fashion*; than which nothing is more becoming the character of a woman of sense and virtue." Benjamin Franklin; emphasis added

"The foundation of national morality must be laid in private families.... How is it possible that children can have any just sense of the sacred obligations of morality or religion if, from their earliest infancy, they learn their mothers live in habitual infidelity to their fathers, and their fathers in as constant infidelity to their mothers?" John Adams

A CHILD IS BORN LEARNING and absorbs everything that happens around him. His mother's voice and touch, his father's attention and care, tones of voice, emotions, or feelings of calm or tension - a child absorbs everything he hears, sees, feels, and senses. What will the child's first lessons be? Hopefully that he is valued, loved, and worthwhile just because he is who he is.

As the child grows and begins to understand language and concept, what are his first lessons? Do they include lessons, both by example and word, of the difference between right and wrong? Is he taught virtue, morality, faith, and all that goes with them? For better or for worse, a child's first lessons in morality are taught in the home. It is from these crucial first lessons in the home that the child gets his first moral bearings. And often the compass is set for life.

Aside from that, where will a child learn morality and virtue if not in the home - from mom and dad, siblings, grandparents, and other extended family? Perhaps in the schools? Maybe from government? Oh wait, perchance prime time TV will teach our children old-fashioned moral values. Ummmm, then again, maybe not.

The *only* place in today's society where we can be guaranteed that our kids will be taught to live a moral life is in the home, with mom and dad's *active* tutelage - by example and precept. Church, extended family, or trusted friends can assist, but the center of the training must be at home. The teaching must be deliberate and constant. Right is right, and it always will be. Wrong is wrong, and it always will be. Decaying societal values, new definitions, and shifting norms do not change those realities.

As parents, we must know and recognize societal drifts and arm our children accordingly. Do we preview required reading at school? If it's not appropriate, do we excuse our children from reading it? My wife and I have done so several times, and our kids were allowed to read other, more appropriate books to fulfill reading requirements. On at least one occasion, other students also brought in different books to read when they saw that our kids were not reading an offensive book. I learned then that we were not alone in our concern for what is being taught in schools. I also learned that when a person stands up for what is right, others will stand up as well.

Television is another problem. How much of what is on TV is conducive to teaching morality to our children? We may tell our children, while they're watching something inappropriate on TV, that what they are seeing really isn't right or good, but in the end it is what we do that counts. By allowing inappropriate media of any kind into our home, we are in essence condoning it. It's time to turn the TV off or to even throw it out, if we don't have the self-control to restrict what we allow to enter our homes via cable systems and satellites.

Instead, we should gather our children around us and teach them the values that made America great. It's time to rear a virtuous generation that can once again thrive under the banner of our constitutional republic.

19
BE VIGILANT

"It may be a reflection on human nature that such devices [as constitutional chains] should be necessary to control the abuses of government. But what is government itself but the greatest of all reflections on human nature? ...If angels were to govern men, neither external nor internal controls on government would be necessary. [But lacking these,] in framing a government which is to be administered by men over men, the great difficulty lies in this: you must first enable the government to control the governed; and in the next place oblige it to control itself." James Madison

"...let them persevere in their affectionate vigilance over that precious depository of American happiness, the Constitution of the United States." George Washington

"The essence of Government is power; and power, lodged as it must be in human hands, will ever be liable to abuse." James Madison

"It may be asked what is to restrain the House of Representatives from making legal discriminations in favor of themselves and a particular class of the society? I answer, the genius of the whole system, the nature of just and constitutional laws, and above all the vigilant and manly spirit which actuates the people of America, a spirit which nourishes freedom, and in return is nourished by it." James Madison

"Of those men who have overturned the liberties of republics, the greatest number have begun their career by paying an obsequious court to the people, commencing demagogues and ending tyrants." Alexander Hamilton

"The aim of every political constitution is, or ought to be, first to obtain for rulers men who possess most wisdom to discern, and most virtue to pursue, the common good of the society, and in the next place, *to take the most effectual precautions for keeping them virtuous whilst they continue to hold their public trust.*" James Madison; emphasis added

THE CONSTITUTION GUARANTEES RIGHTS AND freedoms for American citizens by setting limitations on governmental influence and powers. Why? Why did the founders distrust something as vital as government? After all, a just system of laws is in the public's best interest. So what was the problem? Why so much concern? The answer is really quite simple; government is made up of fallible people. The Constitution was written and adopted to protect us from something that never changes – human nature.

Everyone is susceptible to the allure of power. Consequently, no one can be absolutely trusted when they arrive at the seats of power or influence; thus the caution given to us by Alexander Hamilton: "For it is a truth, which the experience of all ages has attested, that the people are commonly most in danger when the means of injuring their rights are in the possession of those [toward] whom they entertain the least suspicion."

We must be wary of those who overstep Constitutional bounds "for our own good" or out of "necessity", even if, or maybe especially if, we are inclined to trust them. C.S. Lewis observed:

> "Of all tyrannies, a tyranny sincerely exercised for the good of its victims may be the most oppressive. It would be better to live under robber barons than under omnipotent moral busybodies. The robber baron's cruelty may sometimes sleep, his cupidity may at some point be satiated; but those who torment us for our own good will torment us without end for they do so with the approval of their own conscience." (Levin 2009)

Skousen noted that throughout American history, "every unconstitutional action has usually been justified because it was for a 'good cause'.... The whole explosion of bureaucratic power in Washington has been the result of 'trusting' benign political leaders, most of whom really did have good intentions."

Thomas Jefferson also weighed in on the subject:

> "It would be a dangerous delusion were a confidence in the men of our choice to silence our fears for the safety of our rights.... Confidence is everywhere the parent of despotism. Free government is founded in jealousy, and not in confidence; it is jealousy, and not confidence, which prescribes limited constitutions to bind down those whom we are obliged to trust with power.... Our Constitution has accordingly fixed the limits to which, and no farther, our confidence may go.... In questions of power, then, let no more be heard of confidence in man, but bind him down from mischief by the chains of the Constitution."

Therefore, those who claim the Constitution is obsolete or no longer necessary either do not understand why it was written, or they *do understand*, and don't want its limits to apply to them. In either case, we must carefully guard the integrity of the Constitution. We must not be naïve; we must be vigilant.

20
OPTIMISM

"Unless some great and capital change suddenly takes place, ... this army must inevitably be reduced to one or other of these three things: starve, dissolve, or disperse in order to obtain substinence.... Three or four days' bad weather would prove our destruction.... Few men [have] more than one shirt, many only the [half] of one, and some none at all.... Besides a number of men confined to hospitals,... we have...no less than 2898 men now in camp unfit for duty because they are barefoot and otherwise naked." George Washington

"I am distressed beyond expression...for fear that the English fleet, by occupying the Chesapeake, may frustrate all our prospects. If you get anything new from any quarter, send it, I pray you, on the spur of speed for I am almost all impatience and anxiety." George Washington

"Instead of having the prospect of a glorious offensive campaign before us, we have a bewildered and gloomy defensive one...." George Washington

DESPITE GEORGE WASHINGTON'S DESCRIPTION OF the terrible plight of his army, despite defeats, and despite the overwhelming challenges of war with the British and those times when inward worry seemed too much for him to bear, he remained optimistic. Why? What made John Adams declare that though the signers of the Declaration of Independence may "rue" signing it, yet "through the thick gloom of the present, I see the brightness of the future as the sun in heaven"? How was Nathanael Greene able to "...fight, get beat, rise and fight again" loss after loss, until he finally won the campaign in the South and drove the British to Yorktown? (Phillips 1997)

Closer to home, how is it that *we* will find the optimism to resist the current aversion to our founding principles, teach our children the miracle that is America, and steel ourselves for what could be seen as a "bewildered and gloomy defensive" as we seek to put our government back on course? The answers to these questions are the same.

First, the founders had faith that the cause in which they were engaged was just. They firmly believed that the cause of freedom was worth their best efforts and that it was worth any sacrifice they were called upon to make. They were also confident that they were supported in their quest to establish a free government by none other than nature's God Himself. They were sure that the same being who endowed all men with the inalienable rights to life, liberty, and property would sustain them in their struggle to secure those rights.

If we are to have the same level of optimism that our founders possessed, even in the face of great opposition and challenge, and despite the profound personal sacrifice we may be called upon to give, we must be able to answer the following questions affirmatively. Do we have the same conviction they did? Do we believe that the cause of freedom is just and true? Do we believe that nature's God will support us in our struggle to retain our rights and our liberties?

A second reason why the founders remained optimistic is just as crucial to comprehend. In order to understand it, we must become familiar with the fundamental roots of optimism and self-esteem. Optimism and self-esteem come from the ability to face and overcome opposition and setbacks. Optimism and self-esteem are also born of experience with failure, perseverance, trying again, and eventual success.

Unfortunately, as a society, we are teaching our children the exact opposite. Generally speaking, today's parents, teachers, and other caregivers seek to shield children from struggle, failure, competition, and even constructive criticism. The crux of the American self-esteem movement, which really gained momentum starting in the 1960s, is to emphasize how a child *feels*, not what the child *does*. The premise is that if we make a child feel good about himself, than he will perform well.

The problem with this line of thinking is that it doesn't work that way. Kids tend to know when they're not doing well in something, and all the hollow, baseless praise in the world will not change their perception. For example, our child comes home from school and shows us a drawing of a turtle that he made and that he is proud of. When we smile and tell him that it's the most beautiful turtle drawing we've ever seen and that no one could draw a better turtle, he knows that we're lying. He saw all of the other turtles his classmates drew and he knows his was not the best.

Under this circumstance, played out over and over again, the child eventually learns that we are not sincere, that we can't be trusted, and that his legitimate accomplishments do not matter to us. He also starts to entertain thoughts that he and his feelings are not important. The ultimate outcome of this scenario is that the child begins to feel that he, *as a person*, is not good enough. Optimism dies, and negative self-worth is born. When this happens, the courage that most of us are born with to improve and persevere in the face of obstacles (consider a baby learning to walk) dies also. The child will not regard himself as worthy of the effort required for continual improvement. He will also come to view others and his surroundings, including his country, through the same distorted, pessimistic prism. After all, he couldn't possibly make a difference, so why bother? This scenario in all its variations is being played out far too often throughout our country today.

There is a better way however - one that will yield positive returns for the rest of the child's life, and even beyond. When the child gives us the mediocre turtle picture, we express genuine, *realistic* praise and appreciation. "Your picture is very nice. I really like it, thank-you. You should be proud of yourself. Let's put it right here on the fridge so mommy can see it." The child beams because you like his picture just as it is. He then starts to discuss the whole turtle drawing process at school and how Jenny's turtle picture was so good it looked almost real. Then you and your child talk about how he can improve his turtle picture. He puts the tips to use, practices, and his turtle pictures improve; he is proud of *his* accomplishment, even though Jenny's is still better. And even though he's not the artist Jenny is, he has learned that he, as a person, is important and valuable, *just as he is*. He has also learned the value of self-improvement and that he can make a difference for good in his own life as well as in the lives others.

The child learns that he is important, and that he is worth the effort to keep trying and improve. That, over time, translates into optimism and healthy self-esteem; the child learns that despite challenges, he can keep working toward his goals. He learns that his efforts and accomplishments, though perhaps small, will make a difference for good not only for himself and his family, but for the community at large. In essence, he grows into the type of American our founders were, the type of American that we so desperately need today. Optimism cannot be had in any other way.

Research bears this out. When we understand the correlation between low levels of optimism and self-esteem to depression, and then compare that with the rise in rates of depression in the United States, it becomes clear that those generations of Americans who focused on achievement and overcame great difficulty, have greater levels of optimism than do those of us who grew up in relative ease and under the misguided notions and false promises of the self-esteem movement (Seligman 1995).

Depression is on the rise in our country. It is time to get to work and change that. The United States could not have been created by a generation of Americans who were unwilling and unable to face overwhelming odds with optimism. It is time we allow our children to try, fail, try, fail, and try again. Our future generations must know how to optimistically face adversity, just like their forebears, if our freedoms are to survive.

21

THE INDIVIDUAL IS KEY
TO TRUE LIBERTY

"We hold these truths to be self-evident, that *all* men are created equal, that they are endowed by their Creator with certain unalienable Rights, that among these are Life, Liberty and the pursuit of Happiness. – That to secure these rights, Governments are instituted among Men, deriving their just powers from the consent of the governed." The Declaration of Independence; emphasis added

"He that would make his own liberty secure, must guard even his enemy from oppression; for if he violates this duty, he establishes a precedent that will reach to himself." Thomas Paine

"Equal laws protecting equal rights...." James Madison

"Government is instituted to protect property of every sort; as well that which lies in the various rights of individuals, as that which the term particularly expresses. This being the end of government, that alone is a just government which impartially secures to every man whatever is his own." James Madison

THE FOUNDERS WERE VERY DELIBERATE in their wording of such important documents as the Declaration of Independence and the Constitution. They understood the long-standing consequences of their words, and their debates were often long and tedious. For example, during the constitutional convention, the delegates took over sixty ballots before determining how the president should be elected. Consequently, the words *all, created equal,* and *inalienable rights,* can be taken to mean exactly what they say - that each and every individual has the same rights, that each and every individual is regarded equally before God, and that each and every individual is to be treated equally in the eyes of the government.

And yet we are a Republic. And in a republic, the majority sets the policy. As such, Jefferson's words are absolutely true when he says that "where the law of the majority ceases to be acknowledged, there government ends; the law of the strongest takes its place, and life and property are his who can take them." Jefferson was also correct when commenting that "the will of the majority, the natural law of every society, is the only sure guardian of the rights of man." Therefore, our form of government requires that the voice of the majority become the rule, otherwise our rights would be extremely vulnerable and almost certainly trampled.

The concepts of the individual as the key to liberty and that of majority rule may seem to be in opposition to each other. Also, the idea that the majority sets policy may also seem like an invitation for mob rule, and in some ways it is. However, it is precisely because we must have majority rule through a representative government - and in order to curb human nature - that the Constitution was written as it is. The Constitution seeks to balance these two imperatives. If followed *as written,* the rights of no individual citizen will ever be threatened or unjustly withheld, whether or not their views are represented by those of the majority.

The Constitution protects the rights of the individual, and it is up to the citizenry to make sure those protections are extended. If We the People had insisted that the Constitution be upheld, slavery would have been abolished much sooner and without war, the Mormons would not have been driven and plundered, Missouri's extermination order never issued, thousands of American citizens of Japanese descent would not have been placed in internment camps, Woodrow Wilson could not have imprisoned Americans for disagreeing with the draft, and we would have had no need for a civil rights movement or legislation.

It could be said that the Constitution was written not only to protect us from government, but also to protect us from ourselves. If we as a people will uphold the tenets of the Constitution, we will never fear even the smallest infringement upon our liberties, because the intrinsic rights of each *individual* citizen will be protected no matter what his race, religion, political philosophy, or any other characteristic may be.

Thus, one of the inherent duties in "keeping our Republic" is to see that individual rights are preserved as set forth in our founding documents. If the rights of even one citizen are at risk, the rights of all are in peril.

22
UNITY

"I am under more apprehension on account of our own dissensions than of the efforts of the enemy." George Washington

"The present situation of public affairs affords abundant causes of distress; we should be very careful how we aggravate or multiply them by private bickerings.... All little differences and animosities calculated to increase the unavoidable evils of the times should be forgotten, or at least postponed." George Washington

"It is only in our united character as an empire that our independence is acknowledged, that our power can be regarded...." George Washington

"In politics, as in religion, it is equally absurd to aim at making proselytes by fire and sword. Heresies in either can rarely be cured by persecution." Alexander Hamilton

ALL OF THESE QUOTES FROM our founders apply with equal force today. Without question, as George Washington stated, for us "the hour...is certainly come when party differences and disputes should subside, when every man [including those in public office] should with one hand and one heart pull the same way and with their whole strength." Our country and our freedoms are at stake. Again from the father of our country:

> "Differences in political opinions are as unavoidable as, to a certain point, they may perhaps be necessary; but it is exceedingly to be regretted that subjects cannot be discussed with temper on the one hand, or decisions submitted to without having the motives which led to

them improperly implicated on the other. And this regret borders on chagrin when we find that men of abilities, zealous patriots, having the same *general* objects in view and the same upright intentions to prosecute them, will not exercise more charity in deciding on the opinions and actions of one another. When matters get to such lengths, the natural inference is that both sides have strained the cords beyond their bearing and that a middle course would be found the best, until experience shall have decided on the right way; or, which is not to be expected because it is denied to mortals, there shall be some *infallible* rule by which we could *forejudge* events."

Even a cursory review of our history from the events leading to the Revolutionary War through Washington's presidency reveals intense differences of opinion between those who were in reality all "zealous patriots", who only wanted to maintain the purity of the Constitution. Our fight is with those who seek to undermine the Constitution, and not with those who differ with our views on how to preserve it. We must not fall into the trap of having a "bad temper of mind that takes a delight in opposition." Benjamin Franklin said that "in the course of [his] observation[s], these disputing, contradicting, and confuting people are generally unfortunate in their affairs. They get victory sometimes, but they never get good will, which would be of more use to them."

Only through unity and good will can we succeed in the task before us, which is to preserve our Constitution and our freedoms. A large part of that task includes teaching our children, who will learn the skills required for unity from what we *do* much more than from what we say.

It must be remembered that the early patriots, though we have come to revere them, were simply people. They had a common goal but did not always agree on the best way to reach it, including Washington and the military leaders under his command. Yet they were unified. Consider the example of Washington's farewell from his officers after the Revolutionary War was over, as described by Lieutenant Colonel Benjamin Tallmadge, as found in Allison's *The Real George Washington*:

> "We had been assembled but a few moments when His Excellency (Washington) entered the room. His emotion, too strong to be concealed, seemed to be reciprocated by every officer present.

After partaking of a slight refreshment, in almost breathless silence, the General filled his glass with wine and, turning to his officers, he said, 'With a heart full of love and gratitude, I now take leave of you. I most devoutly wish that your latter days may be as prosperous and happy as your former ones have been glorious and honorable.'

After the officers had taken a glass of wine, General Washington said, 'I cannot come to each of you, but shall feel obliged if each of you will come and take my by the hand.'

General Knox, being nearest to him, turned to the Commander in Chief, who, suffused in tears, was incapable of utterance, but grasped his hand, when they embraced each other in silence. In the same affectionate manner, every officer in the room marched up to, kissed, and parted with his General-in-Chief.

Such a scene of sorrow and weeping I had never before witnessed, and hope I may never be called upon to witness again.... Not a word was uttered to break the solemn silence...or to interrupt the tenderness of the ... scene."

We are Americans, first and foremost. As George Washington stated: "We are either a united people or we are not. If the former, let us, in all matters of general concern, act as a nation, which [has a] national character to support."

The words of the master Teacher are fitting, "Every kingdom divided against itself is brought to desolation; and every city or house divided against itself shall not stand." (Matthew 12:25)

Will we stand united or fall divided? The choice is ours.

23
PRIVATE PROPERTY IS CRUCIAL TO INDIVIDUAL LIBERTY

"Whenever there [are] in any country uncultivated lands and unemployed poor, it is clear that the laws of property have been so far extended as to violate natural right." Thomas Jefferson

"The moment the idea is admitted into society that property is not as sacred as the laws of God, and that there is not a force of law and public justice to protect it, anarchy and tyranny commence. Property must be secured or liberty cannot exist." John Adams

"A right to property is founded in our natural wants, in the means with which we are endowed to satisfy these wants, and the right to what we acquire by those means without violating the similar rights of other sensible beings." Thomas Jefferson

"It is sufficiently obvious, that persons and property are the two great subjects on which Governments are to act; and that the rights of persons, and the rights of property, are the objects, for the protection of which Government was instituted. These rights cannot well be separated." James Madison

SKOUSEN, IN HIS BOOK *THE 5000 Year Leap* elaborates:

"[John] Locke pointed out that man received the commandment from his Creator to 'subdue' the earth and 'have dominion' over it. (Genesis 1:28)

"But because dominion means control, and control requires exclusiveness, private rights in property became an inescapable necessity or an inherent aspect of subduing the earth and bringing in under dominion.

"It is obvious that if there were no such thing as 'ownership' in property, which means legally protected exclusiveness, there would be no subduing or extensive development of the resources of the earth. Without private 'rights' in developed or improved property, it would be perfectly lawful for a lazy, covetous neighbor (or the government perhaps) to move in as soon as the improvements were completed and take possession of (or tax into oblivion) the fruits of his industrious neighbor. And even the covetous neighbor would not be secure, because someone stronger than he could take it away from him."

Locke also explains that property is actually an extension of a person's life and liberty:

"Though the earth and all inferior creatures be common [as the gift from God] to all men, yet every man has a 'property' in his own 'person.' This, nobody has any right to but himself. The 'labor' of his body and the 'work' of his hands, we may say, are properly his. Whatsoever, then, he removes out of the state that Nature hath provided and left it in, he hath mixed his labour with it, and joined to it something that is his own, and thereby makes it his property....

"He that is nourished by the acorns he picked up under an oak, or the apples he gathered from the trees in the wood, has certainly appropriated them to himself. Nobody can deny but the nourishment is his. I ask, then, when did they begin to be his? When he digested? or when he ate? or when he boiled? or when he brought them home? or when he picked them up? And it is plain, if the first gathering made them not his, nothing else could." (Skousen 1981)

In other words, property, including the increase derived from our efforts, is a projection of our own selves; property becomes not only ours, but it becomes part of us through our labor. *Labor* can be otherwise defined as what we have done or expended to acquire some form of property, which can be manifest through purchase, sweat and toil, paying others to produce it, or through some other means. Any infringement on our property takes from us a corresponding part of our life and liberty. Supreme Court justice George Sutherland explained it as follows:

> "It is not the right *of* property which is protected, but the right *to* property. Property, *per se*, has no rights; but the individual – the man – has three great rights, equally sacred from arbitrary interference: the right to his LIFE, the right to his LIBERTY, the right to his PROPERTY.... The three rights are so bound together as to be essentially one right. To give a man his life but deny him his liberty, is to take from him all that makes his life worth living. To give him his liberty but take from him the property which is the fruit and badge of his liberty, is to still leave him a slave." (Skousen 1981)

Our inherent, natural (that is, bestowed by nature's God) right to property must be regarded as inviolate. Ironically, the very government whose responsibility it is to defend and preserve our rights to property is the worst offender. It is the government that is bent on either taking our property or telling us what we can and cannot do with it. We, whose rights to property are under attack, must be the ones to resist; We the People of these United States must reign government in. If we won't defend *our own* rights to property from an errant government, who will?

24

SEPARATION AND BALANCE OF POWERS

"These powers [of the federal government]...are so distributed among the legislative, executive, and judicial branches...that it can never be in danger of degenerating into a monarchy, an oligarchy, an aristocracy, or any other despotic or oppressive form so long as there shall remain any virtue in the body of the people.... It is provided with more checks and barriers against the introduction of tyranny...than any government hitherto instituted among mortals." George Washington

"The first principle of a good government is, certainly, a distribution of its powers into executive, judiciary, and legislative, and a subdivision of the latter into two or three branches." Thomas Jefferson

"The great desiderata [desires] are a free representation and mutual checks. When these are obtained, all our apprehensions of the extent of powers are unjust and imaginary." Alexander Hamilton

"I told [President Washington]...that if the equilibrium of the three great bodies, legislative, executive, and judiciary, could be preserved, if the legislature could be kept independent, I should never fear the result of such a government; but that I could not but be uneasy when I saw that the executive had swallowed up the legislative branch." Thomas Jefferson

"It is one thing to be subordinate to the laws, and another [for the Executive] to be dependent on the legislative body.

The first comports with, the last violates, the fundamental principles of good government...." Alexander Hamilton

"The dignity and stability of government in all its branches, the morals of the people, and every blessing of society depend so much upon an upright and skillful administration of justice that the judicial power ought to be distinct from both the legislative and executive, and independent [of] both, ... so it may be a check upon both, as both should be checks upon [the judiciary]." Thomas Jefferson

IN *THE 5000 YEAR LEAP*, Skousen explains that throughout history, governments have typically been monarchies, oligarchies, or aristocracies, with the occasional attempt at pure democracy. While each of these forms of government have their strengths, there are tremendous dangers attached to each as well. For example, a monarchy with its strong center of power is useful for important central needs, such as war. On the other hand, an aristocracy, with its wealthy nobles, will be concerned with protecting the wealth and the development of the nation's natural resources. Both of these areas of focus are important for a healthy nation. However, without restraint, each can (and will) develop into an oppressive regime. As for democracy, the masses may have their say, but the views of the minority have no voice, resulting in mob rule.

In setting up our government, the founders attempted to combine the strengths of the forms of government mentioned above into a stable, workable system. The result of their attempt was the most successful, secure form of republicanism ever known to the world. Our Constitution outlines the three separate but equal branches of government, their attendant powers, and the manner in which each checks the others, with the ultimate power residing in the people. J. Reuben Clark, Jr., a former Under-Secretary of State to President Calvin Coolidge described it this way:

"The Framers...separated the three functions of government, and set each of them up as a separate branch – the legislative, the executive, and the judicial. Each was wholly independent of the other. No one of them might encroach upon the other. No one of them might delegate its power to another.

"Yet by the Constitution, the different branches were bound together, unified into an efficient, operating whole. These branches stood together, supported one another. While severally independent, they were at the same time, mutually dependent. It is this union of independence and dependence of these branches – legislative, executive, and judicial – and of the governmental functions possessed by each of them, that constitutes the marvelous genius of this unrivalled document. The Framers had no direct guide in this work, no historical governmental precedent upon which to rely. As I see it, it was here that the divine inspiration came. It was truly a miracle." (Skousen 1981)

By every estimation, we are the recipients and beneficiaries of a brilliant form of government - one that was intended to place restraints against the human tendency to seek for more and more power. And by and large, it has done so. Despite two centuries of governmental corruption, greed, and power grabbing, our Republic has not yet disintegrated into some form of tyranny or anarchy.

However, the absolute integrity of the separation and balance of power has not been maintained. Presidents have long exceeded their prescribed bounds. A few examples of this behavior include The New Deal, Watergate, asserting that they "will not accept" congressional delay on health care reform, and threatening to pack the Supreme Court so that programs or legislation they desired would not be declared unconstitutional. Congress, for its part, has legislated into existence and then funded agencies that combine the roles of all three branches of government without any checks. The Supreme Court has stepped into the role of legislator, stepping not only on the toes of the United States Congress, but also thwarting the constitutional rights of state governments, local governments, and citizens.

We may be tempted to blame "those corrupt and greedy politicians" for violating the separation of powers and the checks and balances as set forth in the Constitution, and rightly so. However, much of the blame must be laid squarely upon our own shoulders for not asserting our voices, efforts, and votes to maintain the sanctity of the law of our land. It is time for us to hear and heed the caution George Washington gave in his farewell address:

"It is important...that the *habits of thinking* in a free country should inspire caution in those entrusted with its administration to confine themselves within their respective constitutional spheres, avoiding in the exercise of the powers of one department to encroach upon another. The spirit of encroachment tends to consolidate the powers of all the departments in one, and thus to create, whatever the form of government, a real despotism. A just estimate of that love of power, and proneness to abuse it, which predominates in the human heart is sufficient to satisfy us of the truth of this position. The necessity of reciprocal checks in the exercise of political power, by dividing and distributing it into different depositories and constituting each the guardian of the public weal against invasions by the others, has been evinced by experiments ancient and modern, some of them in our own country and under our own eyes. To *preserve* them *must be as necessary* as to institute them. If in the opinion of the people the distribution or modification of the constitutional powers be in any particular wrong, let it be corrected by an amendment in the way which the Constitution designates. *But let there be no change by usurpation; for though this, in one instance, may be the instrument of good, it is the customary weapon by which free governments are destroyed.* The precedent must always greatly overbalance in permanent evil any partial or transient benefit which the use can at any time yield."
emphasis added

All three branches of government have superseded their constitutional bounds, and in the process, our freedoms have been, and continue to be eroded. These constitutional bounds can be likened to banks of solid rock protecting us from the raging river of government. If the bank holds firm, there is no danger of the river overflowing its bounds. But if the hard, outer layer of the bank starts to give way, albeit slowly, the chips and cracks in the once smooth surface leave the bank open to ever swifter erosion. Once that happens, the only thing that can prevent the raging torrent of government from overrunning the fertile fields of freedom are the people who with spades and trowels, step forward as one to shore up the breach.

The erosion began a long time ago and has continued with ever-increasing rapidity and force. Today, some of the last chunks of the protective bank threaten to break loose - they are hanging by a thread. We must grab our tools, hand in hand with our neighbors and children, and get to work.

25

A FEDERAL SYSTEM OF GOVERNMENT

"We are either a united people under one head and for federal purposes, or we are thirteen independent sovereignties eternally counteracting each other...." George Washington

"I confess to you candidly that I can foresee no greater evil than disunion." George Washington

"To the efficacy and permanency of your union, a government for the whole is indispensable." George Washington

"Each State, in ratifying the Constitution, is considered as a sovereign body, independent of all others, and only to be bound by its own voluntary act. In this relation, then, the new Constitution will, if established, be a FEDERAL, and not a NATIONAL constitution." James Madison

IT WAS NOT INTENDED THAT the United States have a *national* government, otherwise defined as a single, central government that sets all policies for the whole. That is the governmental philosophy of dictators and tyrants. Instead, the American system of government is a *federal* system - a system of government in which power is divided between a central authority and constituent political units. In the case of the United States, the power is divided between the federal government and state governments, between the states and counties, and again between the counties and individual cities or towns, all the way down to the individual citizens with their own families and property.

In order for this type of government to function properly, the central government must have sufficient power to regulate the affairs of the whole for the common good. At the same time, the central government must have adequate bounds placed upon it so that it doesn't unduly tread on the powers given to the states and local entities. As Washington said, "It is clearly my opinion, unless Congress have powers competent to all *general* purposes, that the distresses we have encountered, the expense we have incurred, and the blood we have spilt in the course of an eight years' war will avail us nothing." The federal or central government, therefore, must of necessity be stronger than the states, but at the same time, it should not be directly involved "with the particular policy of any state, further than it concerns the Union at large."

It is that balance that must be maintained. To date it has not, and the result is greatly diminished freedoms with ever more blatant and life-altering encroachments looming like a massive thunderhead on the horizon. It is also possible that if the balance continues to shift in favor of the central government, our voluntary, peaceful union of states may not endure.

It is imperative that we restore that balance.

26
Public Officials Are Accountable To The People

"Men in responsible positions cannot, like those in private life, be governed *solely* by the dictates of their own inclinations, or by such motives as can only affect themselves. ...A man in public office...is accountable for the consequences of his measures to others, and one in private life...has no other check than the rectitude of his own actions." George Washington

"That there should be public functionaries independent of the nation, whatever may be their demerit, is a solecism [mistake] in a republic, of the first order of absurdity and inconsistency." Thomas Jefferson

"The natural cure for an ill-administration, in a popular or representative constitution, is a change of men." Alexander Hamilton

"In truth, man is not made to be trusted for life if secured against all liability to account." Thomas Jefferson

PUBLIC OFFICE WAS NOT MEANT to be a vehicle for personal gain or aggrandizement; it is called public *service* for a reason. Elected officials are to promote the best interest of We the People and not of themselves. Elected officials are to be guided in what they do by the will of their constituencies. This does not mean however, that political leaders should bend to the whims and fads that come and go among the populace, especially on weighty or consequential matters. Again we turn to George Washington.

"Whatever my own opinion may be on this or any other subject interesting to the community at large, it always has been and will continue to be my earnest desire to learn and to comply, as far as is consistent, with the public sentiment; but it is on *great* occasions *only*, and after time has been given for cool and deliberate reflection, that the *real* voice of the people can be known."

Never have these words been more true than today. George Washington was calling for public debate and *sufficient time* to gather the true voice of the people, especially on matters of great importance. Currently, issues such as economic stimulus, cap and trade, and health care reform represent major cash expenditures and huge governmental direction shifts and yet the cry has been that we need to do this *now* - that we can't wait for discussion. These issues are so titanic and the consequences of poorly thought out action so far reaching, that no single person or group can possibly know what to do about them, let alone write a well balanced piece of legislation (which won't be read anyway) in the span of a couple of weeks. These issues demand sufficient time for "cool and deliberate reflection, that the *real* voice of the people can be known."

It is time to hold our elected *servants'* feet to the fire. It is time they answered to their constituents once again. It is time to speak up, to demand debate and sufficient time to make wise, sound decisions on these and other issues. We face nothing so critical in this country that immediate, rash action is required. And if our elected representatives refuse to hear us, we must see to it that they don't get a second chance. We must rise up and make it abundantly clear that they will be ousted from power if they don't hear us. Furthermore, our politicians must know that we mean exactly what we say, or they will continue to ignore us.

27

Debt Is A Burden To Be Avoided

"But what madness must it be to *run in debt* for these superfluities!" Benjamin Franklin

"...out of debt, as the proverb says, was being out of danger." Benjamin Franklin

"I wish it were possible to obtain a single amendment to our Constitution. I would be willing to depend on that alone for the reduction of the administration of our government to the genuine principles of its Constitution; I mean an additional article taking from the federal government the power of borrowing." Thomas Jefferson

"As parents, we can have no joy, knowing that this government is not sufficiently lasting to ensure any thing which we may bequeath to posterity: And by a plain method of argument, as we are running the next generation into debt, we ought to do the work of it, otherwise we use them meanly and pitifully." Thomas Paine

GEORGE WASHINGTON, WHILE COUNSELING THOSE of his day, provides apt description of the spending habits of our government today: "There is no practice more dangerous than that of borrowing money...for when money can be had in this way, repayment is seldom thought of in time, the interest becomes a moth, exertions to raise it by dint of industry cease, it comes easy and is spent freely, and many things indulged in that would never be thought of if [they were] to be purchased by the sweat of the brow. In the meantime, the debt is accumulating like a snowball in rolling." The only thing to be corrected when applying Washington's words to our own day is that the "snowball" of his time has grown into a colossal avalanche that has swept over us and will soon crush us. But, "My, the snow is pretty" seems to be the response of most Americans. Besides, snow turns to water, which is pretty important, right? Maybe, but when that much snow melts, we will all drown.

Try as we might to find one, there is no silver lining when it comes to the mountainous debt our government has racked up. Government's irresponsibility is simply beyond appalling. But what about us, the citizens? We have either approved of or stood idly by while *trillions* of dollars have been borrowed. Can any of us even fathom how much money is spoken for through such entitlement programs as Social Security, Medicare, or Medicaid? There is no way to meet our current obligations and yet we continue adding more and more mammoth government programs. Where's the logic?

How have we come to this point? Are we so unwilling to take care of ourselves, or have we developed such a finely tuned sense of entitlement that we're content to have the government provide us with our "necessities"?

Perhaps we're on the verge of bankrupting our nation because we've forgotten Benjamin Franklin's advice on frugality: "When you incline to have new clothes, look first well over the old ones, and see if you cannot shift with them another year, either by scouring, mending, or even patching if necessary. Remember, a patch on your coat and money in your pocket is better and more creditable than a writ on your back and no money to take it off." Then again, it may be that we haven't forgotten Franklin's advice. It may just be that we just think we deserve that new set of clothes.

Whatever the reasons for the massive governmental debt, we now have a choice to make. Either we force our elected officials to stop the insane spending and do all we can to start eliminating the debt - regardless of what it requires - or we keep riding the avalanche until it breaks our bones, crushes our families, destroys the country, and leaves generations of our posterity enslaved by this generation's greed and selfishness.

Jefferson said that each generation is morally bound to pay back their own debts. Will we? Living within our means should be taught at home. Are we teaching it? Politicians intent on reelection will surely hear tens of millions of angry Americans demanding fiscal responsibility. We need to get out the megaphones.

28
Patriotism And Loyalty

"Citizens by birth or choice of a common country, that country has a right to concentrate your affections. The name of AMERICAN, which belongs to you in your national capacity, must always exalt the just pride of patriotism more than any appellation derived from local discriminations." George Washington

"The man who loves his country on its own account... can never be divorced from it, can never refuse to come forward when he finds that she is engaged in dangers which he was the means of warding off." Thomas Jefferson

"The first object of my heart is my own country. In that is embarked my family, my fortune, and my own existence." Thomas Jefferson

CAN EACH OF US, ALONG with Thomas Jefferson, proclaim that "[our] affections are first for [our] own country?" We owe all that we have and are to the United States of America. America deserves our loyalty. She has the right to expect that patriotic feelings and actions arise within us more than just on the Fourth of July or on the anniversary of the 9/11 catastrophes. There are probably those who get more pride out of being a fan of a particular sports team than they do out of being an American. We'll use the Nebraska Cornhuskers as an example. Sure, the Huskers are great to watch; but they don't feed us, clothe us, house us, or protect our freedoms. America deserves even greater affection and loyalty than Nebraskans give their football.

However, there is one thing we can learn from and emulate in die-hard Husker fans: they are loyal. Even after Coach Tom Osborne retired and Husker football began to struggle, home games were still sold out, as they have been ever since 1962, a statistic made even more impressive since the stadium seats over eighty thousand people. Husker fans stick with their team through the ups *and* the downs.

In this regard, we must always stand with Jefferson. We "can never refuse to come forward when [we] find that [America] is engaged in dangers which [we are] the means of warding off." America, and the freedoms she protects for us, are facing great danger. However, we as a people have the ability to ward them off. The question is, will we? Would we rather keep our freedoms or would we prefer the socialized systems of other countries? Would we prefer to keep our sovereignty, or do we want to give it over to outside organizations such as the United Nations? Will we continue to sit idly by while our politicians mock our laws and forsake our freedoms in order to make us more like the rest of the world?

We are *not* the rest of the world! We are *America*! When will we start acting like it? This statement from Thomas Jefferson while he was traveling in France still applies today, and perhaps even more so. "To come here... will make you adore your own country, its soil, its climate, its equality, liberty, laws, people, and manners. My God! how little do my countrymen know what precious blessings they are in possession of, and which no other people on earth enjoy.... While we shall see multiplied instances of Europeans going to live in America, I will venture to say no man now living will ever see an instance of an American removing to settle in Europe, and continuing there."

Let us, with Jefferson, "let the love of our country soar above all minor passions." What's more, let us be what we were born to be: Americans. Let us be loyal and patriotic citizens of the greatest nation on earth. Such devotion is a small price to pay for the "precious blessings [we] are in possession of."

29
The United States Of America Is A Republic

"I conscientiously believe that governments founded in [republican principles] are more friendly to the happiness of the people at large, and especially of a people so capable of self government as ours." Thomas Jefferson

"Republicanism is not the phantom of a deluded imagination. On the contrary,...under no form of government will laws be better supported, liberty and property better secured, or happiness be more effectually dispensed to mankind." George Washington

"[W]e may define a republic to be...a government which derives all its powers directly or indirectly from the great body of the people, and is administered by persons holding their offices during pleasure for a limited period, or during good behavior." James Madison

THE UNITED STATES OF AMERICA is not a democracy. Pure democracy would require that each citizen give his or her opinion on every matter, or at least that every citizen would vote on every issue. Not only is that form of government rather unwieldy in a nation as large and populous as America but, as discussed earlier, mob rule would be the result.

America's form of government was defined by Jefferson as follows: "Governments are more or less republican as they have more or less of the element of popular election and control in their composition..." He continues, "...and believing, as I do, that the mass of the citizens is the safest depository of their own rights, and especially that the evils flowing from the duperies of the people are less injurious than those from the egoism of their agents, I am a friend to that composition of government which has in it the most of this ingredient." Hence, we are a republic. We are a republic where the power resides with the people to hold our elected representative servants accountable.

Jefferson was also of the opinion that the size of our nation lent itself well to a republican form of government. "[The] extent [of the Republic] has saved us. While some parts were laboring under the paroxysm of delusion, others retained their senses, and time was thus given to the affected parts to recover their health." On another instance, Jefferson remarked that "had our territory been even a third only of what it is, we were gone."

I have often been astounded at the unprecedented heights the United States of America has achieved in its relatively brief national history. As I have pondered America's attainments, I have been led to ask how or why? Throughout the millennia of human existence on earth, how is it that our nation has prospered beyond compare? What are the factors that have combined to enable us to lead out in such astonishing technological advances? I do not think we as Americans are more talented or intelligent than those who inhabit other countries, so what can explain it?

While that is a rather broad question and though there may be several interrelated answers, I believe it is largely due to our form of government that America has prospered to such a degree. Because of the freedoms granted by our republican system of governance, Americans are not restricted by the fetters of governmental control or coercion. We have been free to learn, innovate, and improve ourselves. What a marvelous legacy to pass on to our children. However, will we be able to? Is government intrusion now reaching the point where such levels of freedom and innovation will not be possible? Will our children and grandchildren enjoy the freedom to make of themselves the very best they are capable of? The answer to these questions depends largely upon us. The answer depends upon whether or not we will defend and restore our constitutional republican roots.

Let us, as Jefferson counseled, retain (or regain where needed) our senses, and thereby bring our Republic to health once again.

30
BEWARE OF POLITICAL PARTIES

"If we mean to support the liberty and independence which it has cost us so much blood and treasure to establish, we must drive far away the demon of party spirit and local reproach." George Washington

"There is an opinion that parties in free countries are useful checks upon the administration of the government and serve to keep alive the spirit of liberty. This within certain limits is probably true, and in governments of a monarchial cast patriotism may look with indulgence, if not with favor, upon the spirit of party. But in those of the popular character, in governments purely elective, it is a spirit not to be encouraged. From their natural tendency, it is certain there will always be enough of that spirit for every salutary purpose. And there being constant danger of excess, the effort ought to be, by force of public opinion, to mitigate and assuage it. A fire not to be quenched, it demands a uniform vigilance to prevent its bursting into a flame, lest, instead of warming, it should consume." George Washington

"Men have differed in opinion, and been divided into parties by these opinions, from the first origin of societies, and in all governments where they have been permitted freely to think and to speak. The same political parties which now agitate the United States have existed through all time. Whether the power of the people or that of the [aristocracy] should prevail were questions which kept the states of Greece and Rome in eternal convulsions, as they now schismatize every people whose minds and mouths are not shut up by the gag of a despot. And in fact, the terms of Whig and Tory belong to natural as well as to civil history. They denote the temper and constitution of mind of different individuals." Thomas Jefferson

From these quotes we determine that Washington and Jefferson had certain basic views on political parties. They thought that the spirit of party has always and will always exist and that there may be some general usefulness to them. But at the same time, they believed that political parties are a "demon" that must be constantly watched and controlled. Madison paralleled their views in his statement that "the latent causes of faction are thus sown in the nature of man."

Jefferson taught that with all party variances and nuances considered, there are really only two types of political parties - those that trust the people with the power of government and who want the power to reside in the populace, and those that seek to amass governmental power within a central, all-controlling institution or group. He stated it as follows:

> "Men by their constitutions are naturally divided into two parties: 1. Those who fear and distrust the people, and wish to draw all powers from them into the hands of the higher classes. 2. Those who identify themselves with the people, have confidence in them, [and] cherish and consider them as the most honest and safe, although not the most wise, depository of the public interests. In every country these two parties exist, and in every one where they are free to think, speak, and write, they will declare themselves. Call them...by whatever name you please, they are the same parties still, and pursue the same object."

This is not to imply that our current day Republican and Democrat political parties represent the two opposing views Jefferson described. Indeed, it seems that *both* of our major political parties may fall within the ranks of those who distrust the people and are trying to remove the power of government from them. If that is the case, and if Jefferson is correct that both "parties" always exist in a free country, then those of us who are of the "party", or mindset, that the people are the safest depository of the public interest had better step in to fill the vacuum.

However, regardless of any loyalty we may have to one party or another, we should be very careful not to give blind allegiance to any party of political thought or action. Jefferson's practice of political independence is sound advice for all.

> "I never submitted the whole system of my opinions to the creed of any party of men whatever, in religion, in philosophy, in politics, or in anything else where I was capable of thinking for myself. Such an addiction is the last degradation of a free and moral agent. If I could not go to heaven but with a party, I would not go there at all."

31

LOVE THE UNITED STATES OF AMERICA

My country, 'tis of thee,
Sweet land of Liberty,
Of thee I sing;
Land where my fathers died,
Land of the pilgrims' pride,
From every mountain side
Let freedom ring!

My native country, thee,
Land of the noble free,
Thy name I Love;
I love thy rocks and rills,
Thy woods and templed hills.
My heart with rapture thrills
Like that above.

Let music swell the breeze
And ring from all the trees
Sweet freedom's song;
Let mortal tongues awake;
Let all that breathe partake;
Let rocks their silence break,
The sound prolong.

Our fathers' God, to thee,
Author of liberty,
To thee we sing;
Long may our land be bright
With freedom's holy light.
Protect us by thy might,
Great God, our King!

Do we love our country as described in this hymn by Samuel F. Smith? Are we proud to be Americans? Do we want to hear freedom ring from every mountainside? When we contemplate the beauty of what is America, does rapture thrill our hearts? Do we proclaim and prolong sweet freedom's song?

If not, perhaps it is because we have not given enough to our country. Consider a mother's love for a moment. From the first second of life, and even before, she is enamored with her baby. Why? It is in large measure because she has suffered discomfort, changed her lifestyle if needed, thought about, dreamed of, prepared for, endured nine months of anticipation, and in the end suffered excruciating pain, sometimes nearly giving her life so her little one might live. Then she begins to nurture, come to know, train, teach, play with, and work for her baby. She educates herself on motherhood, gives up her own comforts and desires, her sleep, and even her sanity now and then. A mother is there through the good times and the bad. She consoles. The sorrows and the triumphs of her child become her own. The outcome, the result of her labor, is a love deeper than words can ever describe. In a sense, she has *earned* the privilege of possessing a mother's love.

In many respects, just like the responsibility of a mother to her child, America and her precious freedoms are our charge. Therefore, have we earned the right to love America in the same way a mother earns her right to love her child?

If not, perhaps it is in part because we have not investigated her qualities. Those who play the violin surely have a deeper sense of wonder at watching a performance by Itzhak Perlman than those who don't. Those familiar with the intricacies of physics, the properties of matter, or the order of space are likely to have a far greater sense of awe at the complexities and motion of things than are those who do not have the same level of understanding. Have we learned enough of the wonder of America?

Perhaps we don't appreciate America enough because we have not stopped to think how fortunate we are among the billons of people who inhabit the planet. There are those among us who berate America. There are those within our ranks who apologize for our "arrogance." There are those who consider America to be the bane of the world. Do we speak out and question such outlandish falsehoods? Do we demand that those in civil leadership positions speak of our country with the respect and dignity it is due?

Despite all of the complainers in the world and, sadly, within our own borders, America is still the shining beacon of hope, freedom, and prosperity to all people. Who feeds the world? George Washington said he hoped that America would someday become a granary to the world, and we are. Who has liberated countless millions from the grasp of despots? Regardless of the naysayers' gripes, this nation represents the freedoms that the human soul yearns for. Those who doubt this reality should attend a naturalization ceremony to witness firsthand the tears, emotion, and gratitude of those granted citizenship in the United States of America.

Perhaps it is time we sang with earnestness to our fathers' God, to the Author of liberty, "Long may our land be bright, with freedom's holy light. Protect us by thy might, Great God, our King!" Perhaps it is time we earned the privilege of loving America.

32
PATIENT RESOLVE

"Patience is a noble virtue, and when rightly exercised does not fail of its reward." George Washington

"Tyranny, like hell, is not easily conquered; yet we have this consolation with us, that the harder the conflict, the more glorious the triumph." Thomas Paine

IT HAS TAKEN US MORE than two hundred years to arrive at our current level of disregard for the Constitution of the United States, as well as our current state of general ignorance regarding the history of our founding and the principles of our Republic. That being so, we cannot expect that we will be able to reverse course and get back on track in a few days, months, or even a few years. We have to be committed, patient, and resolute; it will take time, effort, and determined focus and work. After all, our task is somewhat monumental in scope; we need to reeducate and gain the support of an entire nation.

Again, we can turn to the example provided by our founding citizens for courage and inspiration. The Revolutionary War was roughly eight years long, and the Americans were trounced for most of the war - not to mention under funded and ill equipped for all of it. The actual war was preceded by years of struggle for redress of wrongs suffered under the hands of the British Parliament. After the war was over and the United States was officially recognized, the fledgling nation still struggled to survive. Even the ratification of the Constitution did not solve all of the young Republic's problems. Throughout Washington's presidency, for example, internal conflict threatened to tear the fledging union apart and still our American progenitors kept on working to ensure the success of what would become the grandest nation in history.

From the very beginning of our country, concerned citizens have had to resist governmental invasion into the realm of individual rights and liberties. Jefferson observed that "the natural progress of things is for liberty to yield and government to gain ground." Consequently, the difficulty of our task today lies in the fact that we have decades of governmental encroachment upon our freedoms to overcome. The enormity of this undertaking is compounded by widespread apathy and the unhealthy sense of entitlement felt by many Americans, both of which continue to be fostered by our current nanny state.

Even in Jefferson's day, the federal government was trying to step into the affairs of the states. His advice was this:

> "We must have patience and longer endurance, then, with our brethren while [they are] under delusion, give them time for reflection and experience of consequences, keep ourselves in a situation to profit by the chapter of accidents.... But in the meanwhile, the states should be watchful to note every material usurpation on their rights; [and] denounce them as they occur in the most peremptory terms...."

We can wait no longer: the chapter of accidents has grown far too long. The only way to accomplish the work we must do is to start at home and with our own families. As that happens all over the country and as families reach out to other families, communities will unite and we will begin to see a return to the principles our nation was founded upon. The more frequent and broad the participation in the crucial causes and debates of our day, the more readily our communities will become vested in the cause of freedom. It may be a long process, but if we endure and continue forward with the patient resolve of our founders, we will reap the same glorious reward: liberty.

33
Freedom Of Religion

"Congress shall make no law respecting an establishment of religion, or prohibiting the free exercise thereof...." The First Amendment

"No provision in our Constitution ought to be dearer to man than that which protects the rights of conscience against the enterprises of the civil authority. It has not left the religion of its citizens under the power of its public functionaries." Thomas Jefferson

"We are teaching the world the great truth that Governments do better without kings and nobles than with them. The merit will be doubled by the other lesson that religion flourishes in greater purity, without than with the aid of Government." James Madison

"The liberty enjoyed by the people of these states of worshipping Almighty God agreeably to their consciences is not only among the choicest of their *blessings*, but also of their *rights*." George Washington

"If I could conceive that the general government might ever be so administered as to render the liberty of conscience insecure, I beg you will be persuaded that no one would be more zealous than myself to establish effectual barriers against the horrors of spiritual tyranny, and every species of religious persecution." George Washington

"...our rulers can have no authority over such natural rights, only as we have submitted to them. The rights of conscience we never submitted, we could not submit. We are answerable for them to our God. The legitimate powers of government extend to such acts only as are injurious to others. But it does me no injury for my neighbor to say there are twenty gods, or no God. It neither picks my pocket nor breaks my legs." Thomas Jefferson

"Almighty God hath created the mind free, and manifested his supreme will that free it shall remain by making it altogether insusceptible of restraint.... All attempts to influence it by temporal punishments or burdens, or by civil incapacitations, tend only to beget habits of hypocrisy and meanness, and are a departure from the plan of the Holy Author of our religion, who, being Lord both of body and mind, yet chose not to propagate it by coercions on either, as was in his almighty power to do, but to extend it by its influence on reason alone." Thomas Jefferson

"Religious bondage shackles and debilitates the mind and unfits it for every noble enterprise, every expanded prospect." James Madison

"Among the most inestimable of our blessings...is that of liberty to worship our Creator in the way we think most agreeable to His will; a liberty deemed in other countries incompatible with good government, and yet proved by our experience to be its best support." Thomas Jefferson

AGAIN WE REPEAT THE OPENING lines of the first amendment: "Congress shall make no law respecting an establishment of religion, *or prohibiting the free exercise thereof....*" Accordingly, any rules or laws prohibiting, for example, prayer or Bibles in schools, are a violation of one of our most basic constitutional and *natural* rights. I assume we can trust the founders' views and interpretation on this issue because they are the ones who wrote the Constitution.

As noted in the Bill of Rights, Congress is not allowed to meddle in religious affairs. However, according to Jefferson, the federal judicial system, including the Supreme Court, is also prohibited from interfering in religious matters:

"Special provision has been made by one of the amendments to the Constitution, which expressly declares that 'Congress shall make no law respecting an establishment of religion, or prohibiting the free exercise thereof...,' thereby guarding in the same sentence, and under the same words, the freedom of religion, of speech, and of the press, insomuch that whatever violates either throws down the sanctuary which covers the others; and that libels, falsehood, and defamation, equally with heresy and false religions, *are withheld from the cognizance of federal tribunals.*" emphasis added

We also know that the executive branch cannot make laws concerning anything, including religion. Therefore, the entire federal government "shall make no law respecting the establishment of religion, or prohibiting the free exercise there of...."

So, the federal government is not to favor or endorse any specific religion over another nor is it to make any laws or rulings respecting the establishment of religion. But neither is the government to restrict or discourage the practice and promulgation of religion in the public generally, and this because it is in the people's best interest to be religious. As an example, Jefferson described an arrangement that was worked out in Charlottesville:

"In our village of Charlottesville, there is a good degree of religion, with a small spice only of fanaticism. We have four sects, but without either church or meeting-house. The court-house is the common temple, one Sunday in the month to each. Here, Episcopalian and Presbyterian, Methodist and Baptist, meet together, join in hymning their Maker, listen with attention and devotion to each others' preachers, and all mix in society with perfect harmony."

It seems odd that churches could share a courthouse for Sunday worship service and not violate the Constitution, and yet a prayer at a graduation ceremony or a manger scene on public property does. It appears that once again, the federal government has stepped well beyond its constitutional bounds, in this instance by seeking to curtail religious expression and practice. Such governmental hostility toward religion is truly ironic when one considers that the founders themselves promoted religion in public life. The founders' views on this subject make perfect sense in light of the realities that religion promotes virtue among the populace, and that a virtuous and moral society is required to allow a government of, by, and for the people to flourish.

For government to restrict religion in a country founded upon the inalienable rights bestowed by nature's God - not to mention the flagrant violation of the Bill of Rights while they're at it - seems a little self-defeating. For the American people to passively allow such a violation, or worse yet to accept and embrace it, is akin to rejecting outright one of our most fundamental liberties. Indeed, allowing the government to unlawfully restrict religious practice opens the door for further restrictions upon, or even outright denial of our other essential rights. Such allowances for governmental indiscretion actually place the entire structure of our constitutional government at risk. Is that really what we want for our children?

34
BEWARE OF THE PRESS

"There is so little dependence on newspaper publications, which take whatever complexion the editors please to give them, that persons at a distance, who have no other means of information, are oftentimes at a loss to form an opinion on the most important occurrences." George Washington

"Printers are educated in the belief that when men differ in opinion, both sides ought equally to have the advantage of being heard by the public; and that when truth and error have fair play, the former is always an overmatch for the latter. Hence they cheerfully serve all contending writers that pay them well, without regarding on which side they are of the question in dispute." Benjamin Franklin

"I deplore...the putrid state into which our newspapers have passed, and the malignity, the vulgarity, and mendacious spirit of those who write for them; and I enclose you a recent sample, the production of a New England judge, as a proof of the abyss of degradation into which we are fallen. These ordures are rapidly depraving the public taste, and lessening its relish for sound food. As vehicles of information, and a curb on our functionaries, they have rendered themselves useless by forfeiting all title to belief." Thomas Jefferson

THERE ARE THOSE WHO MAY feel that the founders, though possibly great and brilliant people, lived in such a distant era that they couldn't possibly be a reliable source of guidance for our current affairs. I heartily disagree. True, they may have just walked out the door to go work on the farm with crude implements, while we jump in the car to go sit in front of a computer surrounded by the latest technological gadgets, but those differences are just in the details. Like us, the Americans of 250 years ago were concerned about providing for their families and about keeping government under control. They were even concerned about biased, unethical media.

Jefferson lamented that he and twenty aids would be unable to answer all of the "calumnies" that newspapers printed about him. Washington expressed similar concerns: "If the government and the officers of it are to be the constant theme for newspaper abuse, and this too without condescending to investigate the motives or the facts, it will be impossible, I conceive, for any man living to manage the helm or to keep the machine together."

Benjamin Franklin, while expressing the need for a good newspaper in Pennsylvania, even listed off the qualities a good reporter would have, including "an extensive acquaintance with languages, a great easiness and command of writing and relating things clearly and intelligibly, and in few words; he should be able to speak of war both by land and sea; be well acquainted with geography, with the history of the time, with the several interests of princes and states, the secrets of courts, and the manners and customs of all nations."

Yet even with the concern the founders expressed about the media, the need for capable, qualified reporters, and the apparent lack thereof, they recognized the immense power and value of having a vehicle for disseminating information:

> "Freneau's paper has saved our Constitution, which was galloping fast into monarchy and has been checked by no means so powerfully as by that paper. It is well and universally known that it has been that paper which has checked the career of the monocrats." Thomas Jefferson

> "The basis of our governments being the opinion of the people, the very first object should be to keep that right: and were it left to me to decide whether we should have a government without newspapers, or newspapers without a government, I should not hesitate a moment to prefer the latter." Thomas Jefferson

Without a doubt, a free press is essential to the maintenance of our freedoms. However, the media must be read, viewed, or listened to with a discerning eye and a critical ear.

35

THE JUDICIARY

"The legislative and executive branches may sometimes err, but elections and dependence will bring them to rights. The judiciary branch is the instrument which, working like gravity without intermission, is to press us at last into one consolidated mass.... If Congress fails to shield the states from dangers so palpable and so imminent, the states must shield themselves and meet the invader foot to foot." Thomas Jefferson

"It is a very dangerous doctrine to consider the judges as the ultimate arbitrators of all constitutional questions. It is one which would place us under the despotism of an oligarchy.... The Constitution has erected no such single tribunal, knowing that to whatever hands confided, with the corruptions of time and party, its members would become despots. It has more wisely made all the departments coequal and cosovereign within themselves." Thomas Jefferson

"The Chief Justice [John Marshall] says, 'There must be an ultimate arbiter somewhere.' True, there must, but does that prove it is either party? The ultimate arbiter is the people of the Union, assembled by their deputies in convention at the call of Congress or of two-thirds of the states." Thomas Jefferson

"In the first place, there is not a syllable in the plan under consideration which directly empowers the national courts to construe the laws according to the spirit of the Constitution, or which gives them any greater latitude in this respect than may be claimed by the courts of every State." Alexander Hamilton

WHILE ALL THREE BRANCHES OF government have overstepped their bounds and encroached upon the rights of the states and the people, to date the judiciary has been the most troubling. It has been the judiciary that has gone the farthest in ignoring and violating the separation and balance of powers between the three branches of government as prescribed in the Constitution. Jefferson described the judiciary as a "subtle corps of sappers and miners constantly working underground to undermine the foundations of our confederated fabric." In fact, it is clear from the writings of Jefferson that the Supreme Court wasted no time in exceeding the powers allotted to them. "After twenty years' confirmation of the federal system by the voice of the nation, declared through the medium of elections, we find the judiciary on every occasion still driving us into consolidation." In other words, within twenty years after the ratification of the Constitution, the Supreme Court's practices were already threatening our federal system's balance of power between the central, state, and local governments.

Part of the reason for this is the manner in which the judiciary was established. Both the executive and the legislative branches are elected by the people, and their members must seek re-election when their terms of office expire if they wish to continue in their offices. They are accountable to the people. Supreme Court justices, however, are not; they are appointed for life, contingent upon good behavior. A probable reason for this is found in Washington's view that the judiciary should be "independent in its operations." However Washington also said that the court should be "as perfect as possible in its formation." The Constitution did place a check on Supreme Court justices by providing for an impeachment process, although Jefferson described it as not even a "scarecrow" - such an obscure threat that the judges felt completely secure in their appointments and therefore free from any restraints. After some experience with the court, Jefferson also lamented that they had not set term limits for the Supreme Court judges, such that there might have been greater incentive for the Supreme Court to operate within the confines of the Constitution.

The idea of judicial review is also problematic. Jefferson actually declared it unconstitutional, saying that the Court could only determine the constitutionality of laws pertaining to its jurisdiction. According to Jefferson, the courts were *not* permitted to determine the constitutionality of laws that fell to the realm of the executive or legislative branches. Such a determination was left for each of the respective branches of government to determine for themselves. So, for instance, a decision of the President on the constitutionality of a law respecting his office could not be overruled by either of the other branches, including the Supreme Court. Otherwise, the Supreme Court would be rendered more powerful than the executive, subverting the constitutional system of separate but equal branches of government. In the same vein, the Court cannot order either of the other two branches of government to fulfill their duties, as neither is subordinate to the Court.

The Constitution enumerates the exact powers set apart for the Supreme Court. Basically, the Court rules on questions involving maritime law, controversies involving ambassadors or other public ministers, in instances where the United States is a party in the conflict, and in *inter*state issues. Nowhere in the Constitution is the Court given jurisdiction to rule on cases that involve issues confined to the citizens of a single state.

In addition, the Constitution does not give any branch of the federal government, including the Supreme Court, any authority to deal with issues of religion. Therefore, under the protections afforded the states in the tenth amendment, it appears that the Supreme Court should neither be involved in, nor rule on matters of religion, including prayer in schools or displaying the ten commandments in a state capitol; those issues are to be left for the states to decide. If not, and if the Supreme Court rules where it has no constitutional authority, then, in the words of Thomas Jefferson, the Court continues to construe "our Constitution...of a general [or federal] and special [or state] government to a general and supreme one alone. This will lay all things at their feet...."

Lino A. Graglia, Dalton Cross Professor of Law at the University of Texas, described some of the more recent usurpations of power by the Supreme Court as follows:

> "Purporting merely to enforce the Constitution, the Supreme Court has for some thirty years usurped and exercised legislative powers that its predecessors could not have dreamed of, making itself the most powerful and important institution of government in regard to the nature and quality of life in our society....
>
> "It has literally decided issues of life and death, removing from the states the power to prevent or significantly restrain the practice of abortion, and, after effectively prohibiting capital punishment for

two decades, now imposing such costly and time-consuming restrictions on its use as almost to amount to prohibition.

"In the area of morality and religion, the Court has removed from both the federal and state government nearly all power to prohibit the distribution and sale or exhibition of pornographic materials.... It has prohibited the states from providing for prayer or Bible-reading in the public schools.

"The Court has created for criminal defendants rights that do not exist under any other system of law – for example, the possibility of almost endless appeals with all costs paid by the state – and which have made the prosecution and conviction of criminals so complex and difficult as to make the attempt frequently seem not worthwhile. It has severely restricted the power of the states and cities to limit marches and other public demonstrations and otherwise maintain order in the streets and other public places." (Benson 1986)

We must beware of the courts, and especially of the Supreme Court, which almost from its inception has sought to exceed the confines placed upon it by the very document its judges have sworn to uphold with the following oath:

"I, [NAME], do solemnly swear (or affirm) that I will administer justice without respect to persons, and do equal right to the poor and to the rich, and that I will faithfully and impartially discharge and perform all the duties incumbent upon me as [TITLE] under the Constitution and laws of the United States. So help me God."

We must heed the warning of Thomas Jefferson: "A judiciary independent of a king or executive alone is a good thing; but independence of the will of the nation is a solecism [mistake], at least in a republican government."

36
GOVERNMENT OF LAW – NOT OF MEN

"We have probably had too good an opinion of human nature in forming our confederation. Experience has taught us that men will not adopt and carry into execution measures the best calculated for their own good without the intervention of a coercive power." George Washington

"Even the best of men in authority are liable to be corrupted by passion. We may conclude then that the law is reason without passion, and it is therefore preferable to any individual." Aristotle

"That love of order and obedience to the laws which so remarkably characterize the citizens of the United States are sure pledges of internal tranquility." Thomas Jefferson

"If it be asked, What is the most sacred duty and the greatest source of our security in a Republic? The answer would be, An inviolable respect for the Constitution and Laws – the first growing out of the last.... A sacred respect for the constitutional law is the vital principle, the sustaining energy of a free government." Alexander Hamilton

"But where, says some, is the King of America? I'll tell you Friend, he reigns above, and doth not make havoc of mankind like the Royal Brute of Britain...let it be brought forth placed on the divine law, the word of God; let a crown be placed thereon, by which the world may know, that so far as we approve of monarchy, that in America the law is king." Thomas Paine

To be governed by sound law to which every citizen is subject yields stability. To be governed by the whims of men means that with every election we have in this country, the rules change. The founders were fully aware of the dangers that come with a government of fallible human beings. They knew full well that a government subject to the capriciousness of men would quickly erode the freedoms they had just purchased with their blood. Thus, the Constitution was established. It was intended to be a law that would stand forever, and to which *every single person* that would ever live in America would be subject, including the President of the United States himself.

The problem is that there are many in government who do not follow the law, and we have not held them accountable. The courts have overstepped their bounds, thereby breaking the supreme law of the land and Congress has done the same. Presidents past and present disregard the law to suit their pleasure. People who cheat on their taxes are appointed to positions of power without being subject to the same penalties every other American would be subject to.

With the signing of the Magna Carta, even the King of England became subject to law. We do not have a king in this country: we have elected officials whose power is temporary and comes from us. If *anyone* should follow the law completely, it is those who are (or at least should be) serving with the public trust. When we consider illegal immigrants, dishonest Congressmen, Presidents who commit perjury under oath, Supreme Court Justices who place personal belief above the standard they are to judge by, and so on, we are led to wonder if we are still a society of actual law, or if the whims of those in power is now the standard we are to follow.

If we are indeed shifting toward the latter, the endurance of our freedoms is at stake. John Adams declared that "no man will contend that a nation can be free that is not governed by fixed laws. All other government than that of permanent known laws is the government of mere will and pleasure."

Another issue we face with our "government of laws" was described by James Madison:

> "It will be of little avail to the people that the laws are made by men of their own choice if the laws be so voluminous

that they cannot be read, or so incoherent that they cannot be understood; if they be repealed or revised before they are promulgated, or undergo such incessant changes that no man, who knows what the law is today, can guess what it will be tomorrow. Law is defined to be a rule of action; but how can that be a rule, which is little known and less fixed?"

Our tax code is several thousand pages long and changes every year. Representative Richard K. Armey, in a statement he made to the Committee on Ways and Means on April 15, 1997, said that taxpayers spend 5.4 billion hours every year just trying to comply with it, which is "more than all the man-hours used in the entire automotive industry in America." Armey continued, "According to the Tax Foundation, our income tax system alone imposes $157 billion of compliance costs on the economy. This is not the money sent to Washington. Nor is it the amount of foregone economic growth. It is the cost of the lawyers, accountants, lobbyists, tax preparers, and man-hours needed to comply with the current tax code."

The recent climate change/cap and trade bill, formally known as the Waxman-Markey American Clean Energy And Security Act of 2009 passed by the House of Representatives this year, is more than thirteen hundred pages long. The health care bill under consideration in the House is similarly huge and the recent "stimulus" package was also hefty - and all of them unread by our lawmakers. Congress is passing laws without even knowing what is in them. The complications of that irresponsible practice are many.

We, the American people are not as Walter Lippmann and other early twentieth century progressives believed us to be. We are not "mentally children or barbarians," nor do we need so called experts to make difficult decisions for us or to take us by the hand and spoon-feed us because we can't figure out the issues of the day for ourselves (Goldberg 2007). What we need is a coherent, rational system of sound law to which everyone is subject.

As citizens, we must study the issues of the day, add our influence and opinions to the debates, and insist that *every* American abide by the law.

37
THE OBJECT OF GOVERNMENT

"The equal rights of man and the happiness of every individual are now acknowledged to be the *only legitimate objects of government*. Modern times have...discovered the only device by which these rights can be secured, to wit: government by the people, acting not in person but by representatives chosen by themselves, that is to say, by every man of ripe years and sound mind who contributes either by his purse or person to the support of his country." Thomas Jefferson; emphasis added

"The aggregate happiness of the society, which is best promoted by the practice of a virtuous policy, is, or ought to be, the end of all government." George Washington

"Government is instituted for the common good; for the protection, safety, prosperity, and happiness of the people; and not for profit, honor, or private interest of any one man, family, or class of men...." John Adams

"It is too early for politicians to presume on our forgetting that the public good, the real welfare of the great body of the people, is the supreme object to be pursued; and that no form of government whatever has any other value than as it may be fitted for the attainment of this object." James Madison

BY SAYING THAT THE ONLY legitimate object of government is to provide for the happiness and welfare of man, the founders of our nation were *not* saying that happiness comes from "stuff" that the government "gives" us. They did not believe that happiness comes from the government providing

96

for us what we should provide for ourselves. Included in this category are things like health care, retirement monies, prescription drugs, food, rent, housing, daycare, college tuition, transportation, or unemployment benefits. The founders, in fact, were asserting the exact opposite.

Happiness comes from the full exercise of one's inalienable rights: life, liberty, and property (the pursuit of happiness). Government is to secure those rights for all, but it cannot and should not seek to provide for equal results. We do not have a right to health care. We do not have a right to owning our own home. We do not have the right to retire at age sixty-five. These are things that we can aspire to, if we choose, through the application of our inherent rights, individual talents, and good old-fashioned hard work.

The object of legitimate government, is to protect our ability to make of ourselves whatever we choose given our individual drive, abilities, and circumstances. Any governmental attempt to do more or less than this one basic function is a violation of our inalienable rights, and therefore a violation of the Constitution, which is the supreme law of our land.

38
SELF-RELIANCE

"In short, the way to wealth, if you desire it, is as plain as the way to market. It depends chiefly on two words, *industry* and *frugality*; that is, waste neither *time* nor *money*, but make the best use of both. Without industry and frugality nothing will do, and with them everything." Benjamin Franklin

"...care and industry seem absolutely necessary to our wellbeing. They should therefore have every encouragement we can invent, and not one motive to diligence be subtracted; and the support of the poor should not be by maintaining them in idleness, but by employing them in some kind of labor suited to their abilities of body...." Benjamin Franklin

"It is a part of the American character to consider nothing as desperate; to surmount every difficulty by resolution and contrivance. In Europe there are shops for every want. Its inhabitants therefore have no idea that their wants can be furnished otherwise. Remote from all other aid, we are obliged to invent and execute; to find means within ourselves, and not to lean on others." Thomas Jefferson

"I wish they were benefited by this generous provision in any degree equal to the good intention with which it was made, and is continued; but I fear the giving mankind a dependence on anything for support, in age or sickness, besides industry and frugality during youth and health, tends to flatter our natural indolence, to encourage idleness and prodigality, and thereby to promote and

increase poverty, the very evil it was intended to cure; thus multiplying beggars instead of diminishing them."
Benjamin Franklin

FROM OUR VERY ROOTS, AMERICANS are, or should be, a self-reliant people. The very first of our American forebears, who came here seeking rewards ranging from religious freedom to adventure and glory, had to rely upon themselves. They worked and made do, and in time, they prospered. True individual, as well as national freedom comes from being dependant upon no one and nothing, including and especially government.

Americans also sustain themselves and each other, and therefore we willingly help those who are in need. However that help is generally temporary, because the help given is of the type that puts the needy firmly on the path toward self-reliance.

Contrary to the thinking of some, the poor are not entitled to everything the wealthy or the middle classes have. They are not even entitled to what those who are not quite so poor have. Adequate food, clothing, shelter, and an honest means to sustain oneself and one's family should suffice. An upright person is more content with having sufficient for his needs and providing for himself than with having relative abundance that is provided by others.

It is also true that providing something for nothing (or next to nothing) does the recipient no favor. The following by Benjamin Franklin, provides proper illumination:

> "In my youth I traveled much, and I observed in different countries that the more public provisions were made for the poor, the less they provided for themselves, and of course became poorer. And, on the contrary, the less was done for them, the more they did for themselves, and became richer. There is no country in the world where so many provisions are established for them [as in England]; so many hospitals to receive them when they are sick or lame, founded and maintained by voluntary charities; so many almshouses for the aged of both sexes, together with a solemn general law made by the rich to subject their estates to a heavy tax for the support of the poor. Under all these obligations, are our poor modest, humble, and thankful? And do they use their best endeavors to maintain themselves, and lighten our shoulders of this burden? On

the contrary, I affirm there is no country in the world in which the poor are more idle, dissolute, drunken, and insolent. The day you passed that act, you took away from before their eyes the greatest of all inducements to industry, frugality, and sobriety, by giving them a dependence on somewhat else than a careful accumulation during youth and health, for support in age or sickness.

"In short, you offered a premium for the encouragement of idleness, and you should not now wonder that it has had its effect in the increase of poverty. Repeal that law, and you will soon see a change in their manners. *Saint Monday* and *Saint Tuesday* will soon cease to be holidays. *Six days shalt thou labor*, though one of the old commandments long treated as out of date, will again be looked upon as a respectable precept; industry will increase, and with it plenty among the lower people; their circumstances will mend, and more will be done for their happiness by injuring them to provide for themselves than could be done by dividing all your estates among them."

Are we becoming the England described above? Is America trading in the self-sufficiency of her citizens for a dependent sense of entitlement? Even good intent does not justify unwise action. Hindsight bears out the wisdom of our founders on this subject.

Franklin also said, "I am for doing good to the poor, but I differ in opinion about the means. I think the best way of doing good to the poor is not making them easy *in* poverty, but leading or driving them *out* of it." The poorest person who provides for himself is more honorable then he who obtains great heights or riches on the charity of others.

We are Americans. We should relish in, and take advantage of the freedoms we have to make of ourselves the very best we can (and not just monetarily speaking). We must become self-reliant, both as individuals and as a people.

39
THE RIGHT TO KEEP AND BEAR ARMS

"A well regulated Militia, being necessary to the security of a free State, the right of the people to keep and bear Arms, shall not be infringed." Second Amendment

"No freeman shall be debarred the use of arms within his own lands." Thomas Jefferson

"A free people ought...to be armed...." George Washington

"To be prepared for war is one of the most effectual means of preserving peace." George Washington

OUR FOUNDERS KNEW AS WELL as anyone how essential the right to keep and bear arms is. They knew from experience that there was no other means to secure their lives, their liberty, or their property, either from invaders without or from tyrants within. When a thief (or worse) comes knocking at our door, a kindly word or plea for mercy will fall upon deaf ears and a calloused heart. The same is true on the national level. Foreign invaders or terrorists bent on destruction will not be repulsed by flowery rhetoric on the decency of humanity, nor will they be pacified by anything other than total submission to their demands. The strength of arms is not only the best defense, it is often the only defense. If their arms are taken from them, the people are left open and defenseless against threats on both individual and national scales. Washington and Franklin said it as follows:

"There is a rank due to the United States among nations, which will be withheld, if not absolutely lost, by the reputation of weakness. If we desire to avoid insult, we must be able to repel it; if we desire to secure peace, one of the most powerful instruments of our rising prosperity, it must be known that we are at all times ready for war." George Washington

"The very fame of our strength and readiness would be a means of discouraging our enemies; for 'tis a wise and true saying, that 'One sword often keeps another in the scabbard.' The way to secure peace is to be prepared for war. They that are on their guard, and appear ready to receive their adversaries, are in much less danger of being attacked than the supine, secure and negligent." Benjamin Franklin

Of course the question might be asked, at least for the national defense, isn't the military sufficient? The answer to that question is, "Yes, but...." What would happen if sometime it was not? What if defense funding was cut to the point that a strong standing army was not possible or that our military was either insufficiently strong or spread too thin to repel threats to our sovereignty? What if a well-orchestrated, wide spread terrorist attack caught the military off guard? These, of course, are unlikely hypothetical scenarios, but they are possible.

There is also another, more sinister reason why we have the inalienable right to keep and bear arms. Words from the Declaration of Independence explain:

"Prudence, indeed, will dictate that Governments long established should not be changed for light and transient causes; and accordingly all experience hath shown, that mankind are more disposed to suffer, while evils are sufferable, than to right themselves by abolishing the forms to which they are accustomed. But when a long train of abuses and usurpations, pursuing invariably the same Object, evinces a design to reduce them under absolute Despotism, it is their right, it is their duty, to throw off such Government, and to provide new Guards for their future security."

This is a scenario that none of us want and that we all hope and pray will never happen. However, that possibility does exist, and always has, even in the United States of America. If government ceases to protect our lives, liberty, and property, or if indeed the government becomes the chief aggressor in the removal of the people's rights, if the people are unarmed, what recourse do they have to "throw off such government, and…to provide new guards for their future security?" We must not forget, we are a Republic in which the rights and powers of government reside with the people. If such a government does not trust the people to bear arms, that government should surely not be trusted by the people. And when the government actually seeks to impose restrictions on the people's right to keep and bear arms, it is clear that something is out of order. Experience has shown that if there is an imbalance of power between the government and the governed, it will always be in favor of the government. Therefore, we must always be on guard.

The history of our founding perfectly illustrates the absolute need for the right to keep and bear arms. Without guns, the tyranny of the British could not have been overthrown. In fact, the battle in Concord and Lexington, the first real skirmish of the Revolutionary War, the "shot heard 'round the world", was fought to protect the colonialists cache of weapons and powder.

We must never allow our right to keep and bear arms to be taken from us, for without *our* guns, all of our other rights are left to the benevolence of those who still have *theirs*.

40
REDISTRIBUTION OF WEALTH
IS UNCONSTITUTIONAL

"Our wish…is that the public efforts may be directed honestly to the public good,…equality of rights maintained, and that state of property, equal or unequal, which results to every man from his own industry or that of his fathers." Thomas Jefferson

"To take from one because it is thought that his own industry and that of his fathers has acquired too much, in order to spare to others who, or whose fathers, have not exercised equal industry and skill, is to violate arbitrarily the first principle of association, 'the *guarantee* to everyone of a free exercise of his industry, and the fruits acquired by it'." Thomas Jefferson

"If we can prevent the government from wasting the labors of the people, under the pretense of taking care of them, they must become happy." Thomas Jefferson

IN THE SECOND CHAPTER OF this book, Government Gets Its Power from the People, I referenced Chuck, Bill, and the egg-laying chickens. Even though I may think it wrong that Bill is denied eggs, I cannot, with any degree of justification, take even one of Chuck's eggs to give to Bill. And if I, as the inherent possessor of inalienable rights am not justified in redistributing Chuck's egg wealth, then the government certainly cannot do it either.

Skousen explains that prior to 1936, the American courts held that "the expropriating of property to transfer to other citizens was unlawful, being completely outside the constitutional power delegated to the government. It was not until after 1936 that the Supreme Court began arbitrarily distorting the meaning of the 'general welfare' clause to permit the distribution of federal bounties as a demonstration of 'concern' for the poor and the needy."

Prior to that time, the nation had followed the Supreme Court's declaration, that:

> "No man would become a member of a community in which he could not enjoy the fruits of his honest labor and industry. The preservation of property, then, is a primary object of the social compact.... The legislature, therefore, had no authority to make an act divesting one citizen of his freehold, and vesting it in another, without a just compensation. It is inconsistent with the principles of reason, justice and moral rectitude; it is incompatible with the comfort, peace and happiness of mankind; it is contrary to the principles of social alliance in every free government; and lastly, *it is contrary to the letter and spirit of the Constitution."* (Skousen 1981; emphasis added)

President Grover Cleveland also vetoed legislation during his presidency that was intended to use federal tax revenues for private welfare programs. His reasoning was as follows:

> "I can find no warrant for such an appropriation in the Constitution, and I do not believe that the power and duty of the General Government ought to be extended to the relief of individual suffering which is in no manner properly related to the public service or benefit. A prevalent tendency to disregard the limited mission of this power and duty should, I think, be steadfastly resisted, to the end that the lesson should be constantly enforced *that though the people support the Government the Government should not support the people.*
>
> "The friendliness and charity of our countryman can always be relied upon to relieve their fellow-citizens in misfortune. This has been repeatedly and quite lately demonstrated. Federal aid in such cases *encourages* the expectation of paternal care on the part of the Government and weakens the sturdiness of our national character, while it prevents the indulgence among our people of that kindly sentiment and conduct which strengthens

the bonds of a common brotherhood." (Skousen 1981; emphasis added)

It is a violation of our natural rights for government to take from one citizen and give to another. Accordingly, the Constitution does not give the government the authority or power for such an act. And yet our government has done so, and continues to do so, with ever more flagrant abuses of illegal power. To reverse such a determined course of action, if it is indeed reversible, will take a monumental and sustained effort. It will take a nation of Americans becoming self-reliant, reasserting their rights, and requiring government to step back into the boundaries set for it.

41
Maintain Strong Local Government

"I am no advocate for [the federal government's] having to do with the particular policy of any state, further than it concerns the union at large." George Washington

"I wish to preserve the line drawn by the federal Constitution between the [federal] and [state] governments as it stands at present, and to take every prudent means of preventing either from stepping over it." Thomas Jefferson

"It is a fatal heresy to suppose that either our state governments are superior to the federal, or the federal to the states. The people, to whom all authority belongs, have divided the powers of government into two distinct departments, the leading characters of which are *foreign* and *domestic*; and they have appointed for each a distinct set of functionaries." Thomas Jefferson

"The state governments possess inherent advantages, which will ever give them an influence and ascendancy over the National Government, and will for ever preclude the possibility of federal encroachments. That their liberties, indeed, can be subverted by the federal head, is repugnant to every rule of political calculation." Alexander Hamilton

"The powers delegated by the proposed Constitution to the federal government are few and defined. Those which are to remain in the State governments are numerous and indefinite." James Madison

"Our country is too large to have all of its affairs directed by a single government. Public servants at such a distance, and from under the eye of their constituents, must, from the circumstance of distance, be unable to administer and overlook all the details necessary for the good government of the citizens; and the same circumstance, by rendering detection impossible to their constituents, *will invite the public agents to corruption, plunder, and waste.*" Thomas Jefferson; emphasis added

"These wards, called townships in New England, are the vital principle of their governments, and have proved themselves the wisest invention ever devised by the wit of man for the perfect exercise of self-government, *and for it's preservation.*" Thomas Jefferson; emphasis added

THE FOUNDERS, KNOWING THAT THE states and their citizens would lose basic rights and freedoms if the federal government ever became involved with local matters, provided within the framework of the Constitution and the Bill of Rights, a clear distinction between the powers allowed the federal government and the powers reserved for the states. The general breakdown of governmental duties is this: the federal was to oversee foreign matters and issues that involved the union as a whole, while the states were to be sovereign in local matters. Perhaps the following two quotes from Jefferson best describe the need for strong local governments:

> "The way to have good and safe government is not to trust it all to one, but to divide it among the many, distributing to every one exactly the functions he is competent to [perform best]. Let the national government be entrusted with the defense of the nation, and its foreign and federal relations; the State governments with the civil rights, laws, police, and administration of what concerns the State generally; the counties with the local concerns of the counties, and each ward [township] direct the interests within itself. It is by dividing and subdividing these republics, from the great national one down through all its subordinations, until it ends in the administration of every man's farm by himself; by placing under every one what his own eye may superintend, that all will be done

for the best. What has destroyed liberty and the rights of man in every government which has ever existed under the sun? The generalizing and concentration all cares and powers into one body...."

"It is not by the consolidation or concentration of powers, but by their distribution that good government is effected. Were not this great country already divided into states, that division must be made, that each might do for itself what concerns itself directly, and what it can so much better do than a distant authority. Every state again is divided in to counties, each to take care of what lies within its local bounds; each county again into townships or wards, to manage minuter details; and every ward into farms, to be governed each by its individual proprietor.... It is by this partition of cares, descending in gradation from general to particular, that the mass of human affairs may be best managed for the good and prosperity of all."

Does that sound like the description of our government today? Sadly, it does not. Today we have a federal government that extends its insatiably greedy hand into as many aspects of the states' jurisdiction as it can. A relatively minor example of such federal encroachment would be dictating national maximum speed limits in 1974 and 1987. On the more egregious side of the scale, we have the 2009 federal government forcing a state to take "bailout" money it did not want.

Notice that Jefferson referred to the division of power reaching all the way down to each individual farm "that all will be done for the best." There has been recent discussion of smart grids that would allow the government (or its agent) to set our thermostats in our houses for us, as well as providing for "real-time monitoring of each customer's energy use through internet technology" (Gross 2009). Government has even mandated what type of light bulb we can and can't use after 2012. The list of related federal offenses is long and growing. How can some career politician or government bureaucrat possibly know what is best for our individual and immensely varied families?

To highlight Jefferson's view: "Were not this great country already divided into states, *that division must be made*, that each might do for itself what concerns itself directly, *and what it can so much better do than a distant authority*." How can someone in Washington DC have even the remotest idea of what is best for any of the states as a whole, let alone individual citizens? I have lived in the great state of Alaska and have also been to the seat of our federal government. And, though it may come as a surprise to our politicians, Alaska and Washington DC are different in every way imaginable. Aside from two Senators and one Representative, the other 532 members of Congress know as much about how to manage the affairs of Alaska as lifelong Alaskans do about managing the affairs of West Virginia, which happens to be basically nothing. The arrogance of our politicians in thinking they know best how to manage the huge landmass that makes up the United States of America, and that entails such a wide variety of states, is as galling as it is baseless.

Well did John Fiske predict:

> "If the day should ever arrive (which God forbid!) when the people of the different parts of our country shall allow their local affairs to be administered by prefects sent from Washington, and when the self-government of the states shall have been so far lost as that of the departments of France, or even so closely limited as that of the counties of England – on that day the political career of the American people will have been robbed of its most interesting and valuable features, and the usefulness of this nation will be lamentably impaired."

"Lamentably," we are there and much of the blame lies with us; we allowed governmental thieves to rob us of our rights to local and self-government. And believe it or not, Washington is not going to humbly admit the error of its ways, beg our forgiveness, and voluntarily step back from its encroachment on local governments.

If we want our local governments back, and if we think we can do a better job of administering to our own needs than "foreign" bureaucrats, we will have to assert ourselves and rescue our rights of self-government.

42
HOPE

"Will not the all-wise and all-powerful Director of human events preserve [America]? I think he will." George Washington

ONE OF THE REASONS OUR founding generation was able to persevere in the cause of America was that they had hope, a hope born of realism. They knew that their task - that of freeing their nation from the powerful British military and establishing a government of, by, and for the people - was monumental, yet they hoped in the justice of their cause, they had hope in the dedication and goodness of their fellows, and they hoped in the sustaining arm of Providence.

It is hope in the dedication and goodness of our fellow Americans that I wish to discuss here. I firmly believe, in part because of America's tradition of goodness, that Americans are, by and large a good, kind, and generous people. I believe that Americans love their country, their families, their freedoms, and in general, all mankind. It is this we should have hope in.

Perhaps we as Americans have not been the wisest stewards and defenders of freedom. Perhaps we have been apathetic and asleep at the wheel. However, we are waking up. If we, the American people, will reeducate ourselves and return to virtue, igniting once again the fierce flame of freedom within our hearts, we will come together. We will once again unite, and we will overcome this current assault against our liberties as we have always done. That is our legacy. We are a people who rise united to face threats against our sovereignty. It is time to do so once again. It is time to free our nation from the grasp of an increasingly despotic government. I, like our founders before, have the hope that we will.

43
EDUCATION

"Education generally [is] one of the surest means of enlightening and giving just ways of thinking to our citizens." George Washington

"The good education of youth has been esteemed by wise men in all ages as the surest foundation of the happiness both of private families and of commonwealths. Almost all governments have therefore made it a principal object of their attention, to establish and endow with proper revenues, such seminaries of learning as might supply the succeeding age with men qualified to serve the public with honor to themselves, and to their country." Benjamin Franklin

"A nation under a well regulated government, should permit none to remain uninstructed. It is monarchical and aristocratical government only that requires ignorance for its support." Thomas Paine

"Say…whether peace is best preserved by giving energy to the government, or information to the people. This last is the most certain and the most legitimate engine of government. Educate and inform the whole mass of the people. Enable them to see that it is their interest to preserve peace and order, and they will preserve them. And it requires no very high degree of education to convince them of this. They are the only sure reliance for the preservation of our liberty." Thomas Jefferson

FEW AMERICANS, IF ANY, WOULD argue that education is not essential for everyone. However, are reading, writing, and arithmetic enough? Is learning about the environment, the physical sciences, the history and cultures of the world, or current events sufficient? All of these topics are very important and each should be studied. However, this list leaves off at least two very important topics. One is the history and founding of our own country, and the other is the science of government.

> "A primary object...should be the education of our youth in the science of government. In a republic, what species of knowledge can be equally important? and what duty more pressing on is legislature than to patronize a plan for communicating it to those who are to be the future guardians of the liberties of the country?" George Washington

> "It has always been a source of serious regret with me to see the youth of these United States sent to foreign countries for the purpose of education, often before their minds were formed or they had imbibed any adequate ideas of the happiness of their own, contracting, too frequently, not only habits of dissipation and extravagance, but principles unfriendly to republican government and to the true and genuine liberties of mankind, which thereafter are rarely overcome." George Washington

It is interesting to note that many of America's early twentieth century progressive leaders studied political science abroad and they returned self-proclaimed disciples of Bismarck and Bolshevism. The result of their training in anti-constitutional philosophies, as measured by the subsequent loss of liberty, has been catastrophic.

It behooves us, as Americans, to ensure that we and our children are well-grounded in the fundamental principles of American government and history. We cannot uphold, maintain, and defend what we do not know or understand. Throughout this book, we have discussed the encroachments of government into our constitutional rights and liberties, some of which are very flagrant, bold, and entrenched. How do we correct these incursions? How do we put America back on course? Jefferson provides the answer: "Education is the true corrective of abuses of constitutional power."

Education is one of the surest keys to regaining the America our founders knew and loved. It has been said that education is power. Let us ensure that our children have the power to reclaim their heritage as Americans.

44
SMALL GOVERNMENT

"Having always observed that public works are much less advantageously managed than the same are by private hands, I have thought it better for the public to go to market for whatever it wants which is to be found there; for there competition brings it down to the minimum of value…. I think it material, too, not to abstract the high executive officers from those functions which nobody else is charged to carry on, and to employ them in superintending works which are going on abundantly in private hands." Thomas Jefferson

"I am for a government rigorously frugal and simple." Thomas Jefferson

Benjamin Franklin in 1778 describing early American government: "The expense of our civil government we have always borne, and can easily bear, because it is small. A virtuous and laborious people may be cheaply governed. Determining, as we do, to have no offices of profit, nor any sinecures [paid office requiring little work] or useless appointments, so common in ancient or corrupted states, we can govern ourselves a year for the sum you [Englishmen] pay in a single department, or for what one jobbing contractor, by the favor of a minister, can cheat you out of in a single article."

Thomas Jefferson's description of American government in 1824: "I think, myself, that we have more machinery of government than is necessary, too many parasites living on the labor of the industrious. I believe it might be much simplified to the relief of those who maintain it."

IF JEFFERSON CONSIDERED THE GOVERNMENT in 1824 too large and parasitic, and felt that it needed to be simplified for the relief of those who supported it, I can't even imagine what he would say about our government today. Words would probably fail him.

Once again, the advice of one of our founders, in this case Jefferson, is perfectly applicable today: "The multiplication of public offices, increase of expense beyond income, [and] growth and entailment of a public debt are indications soliciting the employment of the pruning knife." Well, his advice is *almost* perfectly applicable; we are past the pruning knife stage. Perhaps a chain saw? Whatever implement we choose to use, it's time to start hacking.

45
THE FAMILY AND ITS ROLE MUST BE PROTECTED

"Marriage, or a union of the sexes, though it is be in itself one of the smallest societies, is the original fountain from whence the greatest and most extensive governments have derived their beings." Benjamin Franklin

"Abstracted from home, I know no happiness in this world." Thomas Jefferson

"If there must be trouble, let it be in my day, that my child may have peace." Thomas Paine

HOME IS WHERE THE HEART is. The home is the foundation of all society. It is where the greatest unity should exist. And ideally, it is a place where a mother and a father combine their unique abilities toward raising the next generation in virtue, respect, and general decency. It is in the home, with parents - and *not* with government, schools, or daycare - that this great responsibility lies.

It just stands to reason that strong and virtuous homes will yield strong and virtuous communities, states, and nations. Again we turn to the observations of Alexis de Tocqueville:

"There is certainly no country in the world where the tie of marriage is more respected than in America, or where conjugal happiness is more highly or worthily appreciated. In Europe almost all the disturbances of society arise from the irregularities of domestic life. To despise the natural bonds and legitimate pleasure of home is to contract a taste for excesses, a restlessness of heart, and fluctuating desires. Agitated by the tumultuous passions that frequently disturb his dwelling, the European is galled by the obedience which the legislative powers of the state exact. But when the American retires from the turmoil of public life to the bosom of his family, he finds in it the image of order and of peace. There his pleasures are simple and natural, his joys are innocent and calm; and as he finds that an orderly life is the surest path to happiness, he accustoms himself easily to moderate his opinions as well as his tastes. While the European endeavors to forget his domestic troubles by agitating society, the American derives from his own home that love of order which he afterwards carries with him into public affairs."

The writings of the founders lend credence to de Tocqueville's assessment. They longed for home when their duties took them away from their families. America's early greatness came not only from the Constitution, but from its families. The early American family worked together, played together, prayed together, and relied upon each other for the success and sometimes even the survival of the family. Parents taught and nurtured their children, and neighbors assisted each other as needed. They did not rely on the government to take care of them, nor did they expect it! By and large, they lived according to Locke's philosophy when he said: "The subjection of a minor places in the father a temporary government which terminates with the minority of the child.... The nourishment and education of their children [during their minority] is a charge so incumbent on parents for their children's good, that nothing (including schools and government) can absolve them from taking care of it." (Skousen 1981)

Today, I fear that many of our families resemble the European families in de Tocqueville's description, more than they do the families of our early American predecessors. I am also concerned that many American parents have forsaken their singular responsibilities in rearing their children. Why have so many of us let the schools, government, media, etc., define the standards that our children will judge themselves against and seek to attain? Why have we let these entities determine the values by which we will raise our children? Why have we let the schools and media give our children such a warped view of America's history, purpose, and government? One need not look very far to see the disastrous results of parents shirking their responsibilities. Unless checked, our weakened homes - and those of the rising generations - will bring about the loss of all that we profess to prize.

Yet we need not despair. Despite the challenges we face in rearing our children and despite the forces that seem bent on undermining the sanctity of the family, we should take hope in the fact that we, as active, involved parents, are still the most powerful influence in determining the moral bearings our children will live by. "Our children take their flight into the future with our thrust and with our aim. And even as we anxiously watch that arrow in flight and know all the evils that can deflect its course after it has left our hand, nevertheless we take courage in remembering that the most important...factor in determining that arrow's destination will be the stability, strength, and unwavering certainty of the holder of the bow." (Holland 2003) This being so, we must exercise exceeding caution that we do not neglect our parental obligations, for the following warning also applies: "Sometimes some parents mistakenly feel that they can relax a little as to conduct and conformity or take perhaps a so called liberal view of basic and fundamental things.... Some parents... seem to feel that they can ease up a little on the fundamentals without affecting their family or their family's future. *But, if a parent goes a little off course, the children are likely to exceed the parent's example.*" (Holland 2003)

According to natural law, we as parents are duty-bound to instill in our children the knowledge, courage, love of country, and virtues required for the maintenance of our freedoms. Nothing we can do is more crucial, not only for our children, but for the entire country. Let us be at it.

46
AMERICA: THE HOPE OF THE WORLD

"It is indeed an animating thought that, while we are securing the rights of ourselves and our posterity, we are pointing out the way to struggling nations who wish, like us, to emerge from their tyrannies also. Heaven help their struggles and lead them, as it has done us, triumphantly through them." Thomas Jefferson

"I shall not die without a hope that light and liberty are on steady advance.... Even should the cloud of barbarism and despotism again obscure the science and liberties of Europe, this country remains to preserve and restore light and liberty to them. In short, the flames kindled on the 4th of July, 1776, have spread over too much of the globe to be extinguished by the feeble engines of despotism; on the contrary, they will consume these engines and all who work them." Thomas Jefferson

"Establishing the liberties of America will not only make that people happy, but will have some effect in diminishing the misery of those who in other parts of the world groan under despotism, by rendering it more circumspect and inducing it to govern with a lighter hand." Benjamin Franklin

"The cause of America is, in a great measure, the cause of all mankind." Thomas Paine

"The station which we occupy among the nations of the earth is honorable, but awful. Trusted with the destinies of this solitary republic of the world, the only monument of human rights and the sole depository of the sacred fire of freedom and self-government, from hence it is to be lighted up in other regions of the earth, if other regions of the earth shall ever become susceptible of its benign influence. All mankind ought, then, with us, to rejoice in its prosperous and sympathize in its adverse fortunes, as involving everything dear to man. And to what sacrifices of interest, or convenience, ought not these considerations to animate us? To what compromises of opinion and inclination, to maintain harmony and union among ourselves, and to preserve from all danger this hallowed ark of human hope and happiness?" Thomas Jefferson

"The last hope of human liberty in this world rests on us. We ought, for so dear a stake, to sacrifice every attachment and every enmity." Thomas Jefferson

"When we reflect that the eyes of the virtuous all over the earth are turned with anxiety on us as the only depositories of the sacred fire of liberty, and that our falling into anarchy would decide forever the destinies of mankind and seal the political heresy that man is incapable of self-government, the only contest between divided friends should be who will dare farthest into the ranks of the common enemy." Thomas Jefferson

WHAT CITIZEN OF THE UNITED States of America can read these quotes from our founding fathers and not feel a powerful sense of gratitude for, and loyalty to our nation swelling within them? Who among our ranks can read these words and not experience a renewed hope in the power of the freedoms we possess? What American can read them and not be filled with a renewed determination to unite in the cause of maintaining our liberties?

We are the beneficiaries of untold sacrifices, that the greatest governmental experiment in the history of the world would be a success. And it has been successful, beyond I am sure even the founders' expectations. Despite the great strides toward freedom that we have seen around the globe, there are still hundreds of millions of people who would give up all that they have in return for the constitutional freedoms we enjoy. We, as Americans today, still share in the responsibility our counterparts felt over two hundred years ago. We, like they, must be true to our Constitution not only for ourselves, but for all who seek freedom, wherever they may live.

And yet there are Americans who, though it defies all powers of reason and common sense, actually *apologize* for America. Apologize for what!?; for being the world's beacon of hope and standard of freedom? It appears that those who do so may be seeking to gain the acceptance or respect of those before whom they lay our nation prostrate. However, such a course will gain them neither. We earn the respect of nations, whether they are for or against us, as we uphold, defend, and live by the principles America was founded upon. George Washington proclaimed that "the virtue, moderation, and patriotism which marked the steps of the American people in framing, adopting, and thus far carrying into effect our present system of government has excited the admiration of nations; and it only now remains for us to act up to those principles which should characterize a free and enlightened people, that we may gain respect abroad and ensure happiness to ourselves and our posterity."

"A city that is set on a hill cannot be hid." (Matthew 12:25) America and her citizens are as a light set upon a hill. May we ever keep her polished and gleaming, that "freedom's holy light" may someday illuminate the entire world.

47

LIVE BY PRINCIPLE

"[Correct principles] ought to be instilled into the minds of our youth on their first opening. The boys of the rising generation are to be the men of the next, and the sole guardians of the principles we deliver over to them." Thomas Jefferson

"Lay down true principles and adhere to them inflexibility. Do not be frightened into their surrender by the alarms of the timid, or the croakings of wealth against the ascendancy of the people." Thomas Jefferson

"In the maintenance of…[our] principles…I verily believe the future happiness of our country essentially depends." Thomas Jefferson

"A departure from principle in one instance becomes a precedent for a second, that second for a third, and so on, till the bulk of the society is reduced to be mere automatons of misery, to have no sensibilities left but for sin and suffering." Thomas Jefferson

"I love the man that can smile in trouble, that can gather strength from distress, and grow brave by reflection. 'Tis the business of little minds to shrink; but he whose heart is firm, and whose conscience approves his conduct, will pursue his principles unto death." Thomas Paine

FREEDOM CANNOT LONG ENDURE UNLESS the principles it is founded upon are cherished, held inviolate, and constantly safeguarded. This is why it is so vital that we know and live those principles ourselves, and that we teach our children to do the same. But even that is not enough. The principles of liberty must become a part of our makeup. We must literally personify the principles of freedom if we are to preserve them. When we actually embody the principles of freedom, we will be alert to any encroachment upon them, and we will not be able to rest until they are secure once again.

In our current era of apathy and sometimes even outright hostility toward the principles of freedom, such a position is not an easy one to take, since a person who does is often labeled a fanatic or worse. However, "it is in vain, I perceive, to look for ease and happiness in a world of troubles." If anyone knew this to be true, it was the man who said it, namely George Washington. Difficult though it may be, we must always remember that "the natural process of things is for liberty to yield and government to gain ground." This statement by Jefferson is glaringly apparent today. The only way to stop the deluge unleashed against our freedoms, is to stand immovable upon the unyielding bedrock of the sure principles which brought the great American experiment to such extraordinary fruition.

Resistance based on principle is our only option. Jefferson teaches us that "when patience has begotten false estimates of its motives, when wrongs are pressed because it is believed they will be borne, resistance becomes morality."

Government persists in its relentless assault against our liberties because it thinks we will continue to bear it. Our principles say otherwise.

48
WORK

"Of all the cankers of human happiness, none corrodes it with so silent yet so baneful a tooth as indolence. Body and mind both unemployed, our being becomes a burden, and every object about us loathsome, even the dearest. Idleness begets ennui (boredom), ennui the hypochondria, and that a diseased body. No laborious person was ever yet hysterical. Exercise and application produce order in our affairs, health of body, cheerfulness of mind, and these make us precious to our friends. It is *while we are young* that the habit of industry is formed. *If not then, it never is afterwards.* The fortune of our lives therefore *depends on employing well the short period of youth.* If at any moment, my dear, you catch yourself in idleness, start from it as you would from the precipice of a gulf." Thomas Jefferson; emphasis added

"Industry need not wish,…and he that lives upon hope will die fasting. There are no gains without pains…." Benjamin Franklin

"Ennui [is] the most dangerous poison of life. A mind always employed is always happy. This is the true secret, the grand recipe for felicity." Thomas Jefferson

"Determine never to be idle. No person will have occasion to complain of the want of time who never loses any. It is wonderful how much may be done if we are always doing." Thomas Jefferson

"He that hath a trade hath an estate; and he that hath a calling, hath an office of profit and honor; but then the trade must be worked at, and the calling well followed, or neither the estate nor the office will enable us to pay our taxes. If we are industrious, we shall never starve; for, as Poor Richard says, at the working man's house hunger looks in, but dares not enter. Nor will the bailiff or the constable enter, for Industry pays debts, while despair increaseth them...." Benjamin Franklin

"Diligence is the mother of good luck, as Poor Richard says, and God gives all things to industry. Then plow deep, while sluggards sleep, and you shall have corn to sell and to keep...." Benjamin Franklin

FOR EARLY AMERICANS, SURVIVAL OFTEN depended upon the labor of the entire family, children included. Often, "the house was every bit...a workplace as the sawmill" (Ulrich 1990).

Generally speaking, this is not the case in America today; our children do not contribute significantly to the family's physical needs. Yes, they may have a few chores, but do they really work? Most of us don't grow our own food, make our own clothes, or even shingle our own houses. So what do America's children do? Pastimes such as watching television, playing video games, surfing the internet, reading books with no real substance, texting, exploring Facebook, participation in sports, wandering around the neighborhood, or just sitting around being bored come readily to mind. While none of these amusements in and of themselves are bad, no one can honestly deny that today's children and youth are generally idle. Their minds, bodies, interests, and passions are not being taxed. In general, they do not contribute in meaningful ways to the support of the family.

If our children are to become Americans capable of maintaining freedom, we must teach them how to work, both physically, mentally, and spiritually. We must stretch them. They must be required to make meaningful contributions to our families and communities. We may say that "back in the day" it was easier to keep kids busy and working, and it was. However, we can't let that excuse deter us; we need to be creative and unfailing in our efforts to keep our kids productive and contributing. Instead of spraying the lawn for weeds, the kids can pull dandelions. Instead of reading *Harry Potter* twelve times, a child can read books on their level about history (there are some great ones out there). Older kids can read classic literature. Instead of aimlessly surfing the web, our children can look up how to build their dog a house and then do so. There are endless opportunities for our children to contribute: we as their parents just need to make sure it happens.

Let us not allow our children to become "sluggards". Life is tough enough, and we do them no favors if we allow them to grow up in idleness. Instead, let us teach them not only to plow, but to "plow deep." This is a vital step in instilling within our children the values and character of our founders. It is a crucial requirement in maintaining our freedoms.

49
Rely Upon Nature's God

"Will not the all-wise and all-powerful Director of human events preserve [America]? I think he will." George Washington

"The foundation of a great empire is laid, and I please myself with the persuasion that Providence will not leave its work imperfect." George Washington

"May the Infinite Power which rules the destinies of the universe lead our councils to what is best, and give them a favorable issue for your peace and prosperity." Thomas Jefferson

"The reformation was preceded by the discovery of America, as if the Almighty graciously meant to open a sanctuary to the persecuted in future years, when home should afford neither friendship nor safety." Thomas Paine

"I consider it an indispensable duty to close this last solemn act of my official life by commending the interests of our dearest country to the protection of Almighty God, and those who have the superintendence of them to his holy keeping." George Washington

"I earnestly pray that the Omnipotent Being who has not deserted the cause of America in the hour of its extremest hazard will never yield so fair a heritage of freedom a prey to anarchy or despotism." George Washington

"It is the duty of all nations to acknowledge the providence of Almighty God, to obey his will, to be grateful for his benefits, and humbly to implore his protection and favor." George Washington

"We have had a hard struggle, but the Almighty has favored the just cause; and I join most heartily with you in your prayers that he may perfect his work, and establish freedom in the new world as an asylum for those of the old, who deserve it." Benjamin Franklin

"I supplicate a protecting Providence to watch over...our country's freedom and welfare." Thomas Jefferson

"If such talents as I possess have been called into action by great events, and those events have terminated happily for our country, the glory should be ascribed to the manifest interposition of an overruling Providence." George Washington

"Having taken care to do *what appears to be for the best,* we must submit to God's providence, which orders all things really for the best." Benjamin Franklin

In 1776, the continental congress set apart a specific Friday to be observed as a day of "fasting, humiliation and prayer, humbly to supplicate the mercy of Almighty God, that it would please him to pardon all our manifold sins and transgressions, and to prosper the arms of the united colonies, and finally, establish the peace and freedom of America upon a solid and lasting foundation."

"I sincerely supplicate that overruling Providence which governs the destinies of men and nations to dispense His choicest blessings on...our beloved country." Thomas Jefferson

"I offer my sincere prayers to the Supreme Ruler of the Universe, that he may long preserve our country in freedom and prosperity." Thomas Jefferson

"May the God of wisdom, strength, and power, the Lord of the armies of Israel, inspire us with prudence in this time of danger; take away from us all the seeds of contention and division, and unite the hearts and counsels of all of us, of whatever sect or nation, in one bond of peace, brotherly love, and generous public spirit; may He give us strength and resolution to amend our lives, and remove from among us everything that is displeasing to Him; afford us His most gracious protection, confound the designs of our enemies, and give peace in all our borders." Benjamin Franklin

"And for the support of this Declaration, with a firm Reliance on the Protection of divine Providence, we mutually pledge to each other our Lives, our Fortunes, and our sacred Honor." Declaration of Independence

LET THE WORDS OF THE founding fathers suffice, and may we do likewise.

50

KNOW YOUR ENEMY

"I have, as you observe, some enemies in England, but they are my enemies as an *American*; I have also two or three in America, who are my enemies as a *minister*; but I thank God there are not in the whole world any who are my enemies as *a man*...." Benjamin Franklin

I APPROACH THIS TOPIC WITH some trepidation. I do not wish to be misunderstood.

As I have said, we are Americans, and we are capable of facing and overcoming any challenge. But will we continue in that tradition? We have overcome obvious foreign enemies, but what about the more subtle and outwardly friendly enemies that we face within our own ranks? Thomas Paine described these individuals as follows: "Interested men, who are not to be trusted; weak men who cannot see; prejudiced men, who will not see; and a certain set of moderate men, who think better of the European world [or in our case the government] than it deserves; and this last class, by an ill-judged deliberation, will be the cause of more calamities to this continent than all the other three."

These internal threats to our freedoms are very real and very dangerous. We need to remember that the government is like fire, it cannot be trusted and we must pay attention! We must beware of those who promote government, or seek to enhance its power, and we must monitor their public actions. We cannot naively say that these things won't happen in America just because "things like that don't happen in America."

Our freedoms are under assault, and they will be taken from us unless we defend them. We must dust off our weapons as contained in the Declaration of Independence and the Constitution. We must use the power of our voice and our votes, our pens and our passion. We must not fail. We must not be the generation that allowed our God-given rights to be usurped while we nervously sucked our collective thumbs.

Part of any good strategy when engaging an adversary is to know the enemy. What are their motives? What are their strategies, strengths, and weaknesses? Are they well-funded and organized? What are the most crucial battles to be won? How effectively do they use the press to spread their message? How successful is their use of propaganda and half-truths?

The list of tactics that follows is purposely given in fairly general terms. The hope is that it will begin discussions among family and friends. If that happens, then all throughout America, people will begin to pay attention, research, and form educated opinions. Their next step will be to join the fight that has already begun against the dangers that threaten to take from us the very liberties that so many have pledged their lives, fortunes, and sacred honor to defend. As you read the following quotes, think about recent examples of governmental action, groups (both within the framework of government and without), and even individuals that fit within each of the examples listed.

> "If, from the more wretched parts of the old world, we look at those which are in an advanced stage of improvement, we still find the greedy hand of government thrusting itself into every corner and crevice of industry, and grasping the spoil of the multitude. Invention is continually exercised, to furnish new pretenses for revenues and taxation. It watches prosperity as its prey and permits none to escape without tribute." Thomas Paine

> "The present Constitution is the standard to which we are to cling. Under its banners, bona fide must we combat our political foes – rejecting all changes but through the channel itself provides for amendments." Alexander Hamilton

> "Government is instituted for the common good; for the protection, safety, prosperity, and happiness of the people; and not for profit, honor, or private interest of any one man, family, or class of men...." John Adams

> "I told [President Washington]...that it was a fact, as certainly known as that he and I were then conversing, that particular members of the [Congress], while those laws [assumption, funding, etc.] were on the carpet,

had feathered their nests with paper, and then voted for the laws, and constantly since lent all the energy of their talents, and instrumentality of their offices, to the establishment and enlargement of this system." Thomas Jefferson

"We should be unfaithful to ourselves if we should ever lose sight of the danger to our liberties if anything partial or extraneous should infect the purity of our free, fair, virtuous, and independent elections." John Adams

"I own myself the friend to a very free system of commerce, and hold it as a truth, that commercial shackles are generally unjust, oppressive and impolitic – it is also a truth, that if industry and labour are left to take their own course, they will generally be directed to those objects which are the most productive, and this in a more certain and direct manner than the wisdom of the most enlightened legislature could point out." James Madison

"It [is] a cause of just uneasiness when we [see] a legislature legislating for their own interests, in opposition to those of the people." Thomas Jefferson

"The house of representatives...can make no law which will not have its full operation on themselves and their friends, as well as the great mass of society. This has always been deemed one of the strongest bonds by which human policy can connect the rulers and the people together. It creates between them that communion of interest, and sympathy of sentiments, of which few governments have furnished examples; but without which every government degenerates into tyranny." James Madison

Now the question: What are we doing about it? Well did Washington say, "It has ever been that the adversaries to a measure are more active than its friends." The same is true today. Those intent on taking our freedoms, as well as those who support them in their efforts, are generally more vocal and active than those of us who are concerned about losing our freedoms. However, I firmly believe - and I hope I am right - that the "sleeping giant" embodied in the Americans who believe in the sanctity of our inalienable and constitutional rights is stirring, and is about to wake up.

When I say "enemy" or "intent on taking our freedoms", I refer to those who support policy and action where the result will be injurious to liberty. That being said, I believe there are relatively few who are actively seeking to destroy our freedoms and undermine the Constitution.

Accordingly, we have two things in our favor. First, surely most of our countrymen who fall into the category of those "intent on taking our freedoms, as well as those who support them in their efforts," do not realize the effect such actions will have. It is probable that they do not know because they have never been taught and thus do not understand the glorious principles of freedom. They have simply never been made aware of them.

Second, there are many Americans who sense that we are drifting off course and about to capsize but they don't know why. Those in this category are the fortunate beneficiaries of conscience, which Jefferson described as "the only sure clue which will eternally guide a man [or woman, or child] clear of all doubts and inconsistencies." To continue quoting from Jefferson, these are the people who heed "the true fountains of evidence [that are] the head and heart of every rational and honest man. It is there nature has written her moral laws, and where every man may read them for himself." They sense something is wrong but aren't sure what the problem is.

If these two observations are indeed accurate, then education is the key, and we can literally save America and our liberty one child, one family, and one neighborhood at a time.

There is another weapon in our arsenal, which we must employ as we battle for the cause of freedom. It is this: the American Republic was founded upon natural truth, which can stand on its own as long as debate is not stifled. Note these three quotes from Jefferson:

> "Truth will do well enough if left to shift for herself. She seldom has received much aid from the power of great men, to whom she is rarely known and seldom welcome. She has no need of force to procure entrance into the minds of men."

> "Truth is great and will prevail if left to herself;...she is the proper and sufficient antagonist to error, and has nothing to fear from the conflict unless by human interposition

disarmed of her natural weapons, free argument and debate, errors ceasing to be dangerous when it is permitted freely to contradict them."

"It is error alone which needs the support of government. Truth can stand by itself."

As we teach our children the truths our Republic is founded upon, and as we reach out to our neighbors and friends, we can do so with confidence. We should not seek to silence debate or discussion. Those who do so have something to hide. Truth does not work under cover, which is the reason why freedom of speech must be protected. Those who seek to silence dissent, discussion, or debate are not working from the standard of truth. The message of freedom is not to be hidden, its voice is not to be silenced.

In addition, the language of liberty is not new. It does not originate from man, nor does it belong to the United States. Ever since man has existed on this earth, the mandate of freedom has thundered forth from the realms of nature's God. Consequently, freedom's wonder has already been proclaimed to the world, its truth already established; the only thing we can add to it is our passion and our voice. We must not allow truth to be disarmed of free argument and debate; truth must have her day in court. If the truths of freedom are spread far and wide, they will prevail. Again, by keeping the discussion alive and thriving, we can literally save America, one child at a time.

It is our inherent duty to do so, as noted by Adams:

> "Government is instituted for the common good; for the protection, safety, prosperity, and happiness of the people; and not for profit, honor, or private interest of any one man, family, or class of men; therefore, the *people alone* have an *incontestable, unalienable,* and *indefeasible* right to institute government; and to reform, alter, or totally change the same, when their protection, safety, prosperity, and happiness require it." emphasis added

In our case, a lot of education and a bit of governmental reform should suffice.

51
A Republic Requires A Politically Active Electorate

"The influence over government must be shared among all the people. If every individual which composes their mass participates of the ultimate authority, the government will be safe...." Thomas Jefferson

"We think, in America, that it is necessary to introduce the people into every department of government as far as they are capable of exercising it; and that this is the only way to insure a long-continued and honest administration of its powers." Thomas Jefferson

"The power under the Constitution will always be in the people." George Washington

IF WE WANT OUR VOICES to be heard by the government, we must be active in the political process at all levels. We can vote, support candidates, learn about important issues, and make our opinions known. We can attend public hearings and other meetings, be involved in political grassroots efforts, and can even run for office ourselves. We the People cannot reasonably expect to maintain the power of government otherwise.

Professor Robert Putnam of the Harvard Kennedy School, measured the decline of civic engagement in recent decades. He reports his findings as follows: "Americans have become perhaps 10 - 15 percent less likely to voice our views publicly by running for office or writing congress or the local newspaper, 15 - 20 percent less interested in politics and public affairs, roughly 25 percent less likely to vote, roughly 35 percent less likely to attend public meetings, both partisan and nonpartisan, and roughly 40 percent less engaged in party politics and indeed in political and civic organizations of all sorts....In effect, more than a third of America's civic infrastructure simply evaporated between the mid-1970s and the mid-1990s" (Kupchan 2002).

We as Americans have failed in our responsibility to monitor the government via our engagement in it, and the results are borderline catastrophic. If we don't want the Good Ship Liberty to sink, it is time to get all hands on deck. If we all man the sails, we will get our ship back on course toward the bounteous harbors of freedom. If not, the cliffs of tyranny await with open and deceptive arms to collect us in their clutches. The choice is ours.

52
Our National Anthem: The Star-Spangled Banner

During the war of 1812, the British captured Dr. William Beanes. Francis Scott Key, a well known lawyer, was one of those selected to negotiate with the British for his release. Key sailed into Chesapeake Bay and boarded the ship where Beanes was being held. Even though Key's negotiations were successful, the British would not allow the Americans to return to Baltimore until they had completed their ongoing bombardment of Fort McHenry, which lasted twenty-five hours.

Both during the shelling and after it was over, Key and his companions anxiously watched to see if the flag, the symbol of their beloved land, still flew. To their immense relief, their flag was still there. Their flag did not fail them: it continued to wave in proud opposition to the attack and eventually in glorious triumph. When the shelling was over, it was with overflowing joy and gratitude that Francis Scott Key penned the words that would become our National Anthem.

> Oh say, can you see, by the dawn's early light,
> What so proudly we hailed at the twilight's last gleaming,
> Whose broad stripes and bright stars, through the perilous fight,
> O'er the ramparts we watched, were so gallantly streaming?
> And the rockets' red glare, the bombs bursting in air,
> Gave proof thru the night that our flag was still there.
> Oh say, does that star-spangled banner yet wave
> O'er the land of the free and the home of the brave?
> On the shore, dimly seen thru the mists of the deep,
> Where the foe's haughty host in dread silence reposes,
> What is that which the breeze, o'er the towering steep,
> As it fitfully blows, half conceals, half discloses?
> Now it catches the gleam of the morning's first beam,
> In full glory reflected now shines on the stream;
> 'Tis the star-spangled banner! Oh, long may it wave

O'er the land of the free and the home of the brave!
Oh, thus be it ever, when free men shall stand
Between their loved homes and the war's desolation!
Blest with vict'ry and peace, may the heav'n rescued land
Praise the Pow'r that hath made and preserved us a nation!
Then conquer we must, when our cause it is just,
And this be our motto: "In God is our trust!"
And the star-spangled banner in triumph shall wave
O'er the land of the free and the home of the brave!

We live in what is irrefutably the greatest, most noble nation that this world has ever known. But will it continue to be so? Alexander Hamilton declared, that "No man in his senses can hesitate in choosing to be free, rather than a slave." Was he correct? What will our choice be? Will we be slaves to our government, or will we throw off our shackles?

We should, with Thomas Paine, believe that "the sun never shined on a cause of greater worth." For, as he stated, America's freedoms are not simply "the affair of a city, a country, a province, or a kingdom.... [They are] not the concern of a day, a year, or an age; posterity are virtually involved in the contest, and will be more or less affected, even to the end of time, by the proceedings now." Paine then concluded his thought, "Now is the seed-time of...union, faith and honor. The least fracture now will be like a name engraved with the point of a pin on the tender rind of a young oak; The wound will enlarge with the tree, and posterity will read it in full grown characters."

That being so, we, as a united people, must not fail to peacefully take off our shackles and hand them back to our government. Government will not readily allow us to do so, and the process may be long and arduous, but we must not fail; posterity's freedom hinges upon our success. We must all have the same courage, determination, commitment, loyalty, patient resolve, and unwavering dedication to each other and to our Republic that our founding fathers possessed, as expressed so beautifully by John Adams:

> "Sink or swim, live or die, survive or perish, I give my
> hand and my heart to this vote. It is true, indeed, that in
> the beginning we aimed not at independence. But there's
> a Divinity that shapes our ends.... Why, then, should we
> defer the Declaration?... You and I, indeed, may rue it.
> We may not live to see the time when this Declaration

shall be made good. We may die; die Colonists, die slaves, die, it may be, ignominiously and on the scaffold.

"Be it so. Be it so.

"If it be the pleasure of Heaven that my country shall require the poor offering of my life, the victim shall be ready.... But while I do live, let me have a country, or at least the hope of a country, and that a free country.

"But whatever may be our fate, be assured...that this Declaration will stand. It may cost treasure, and it may cost blood, but it will stand and it will richly compensate for both.

"Through the thick gloom of the present, I see the brightness of the future as the sun in heaven. We shall make this a glorious, an immortal day. When we are in our graves, our children will honor it. They will celebrate it with thanksgiving, with festivity, with bonfires, and illuminations....

"Before God, I believe the hour is come. My judgment approves this measure, and my whole heart is in it. All that I have, and all that I am, and all that I hope, in this life, I am now ready here to stake upon it; and I leave off as I began, that live or die, survive or perish, I am for the Declaration. It is my living sentiment, and by the blessing of God it shall be my dying sentiment. Independence now, and Independence forever."

In his treatise *Rights of Man*, Thomas Paine said that "a little matter will move a party, but it must be something great that moves a nation." It is also true that by small means are great things brought to pass. Our "something great" needs to be a resurgent return to the principles of our founding, and it will be accomplished by the small means of gathering our children around us and instilling in them, through word and deed, a love of liberty.

Let us, with Adams, be for the Declaration. Let us be for the Constitution. Let us educate ourselves, our children, and our grandchildren. May the rising generations be well versed in the principles of liberty, and may freedom flow through their veins. May we affirmatively answer Benjamin Franklin's challenge and "keep our Republic."

Let us once again connect with our neighbors and communities. Let us follow the example given to us by generations of Americans past and let us unite in the cause of freedom. Let us be a virtuous and a moral people.

Let us give new meaning to the last verse of our national anthem:

> Oh, thus be it ever, when the free men shall stand
> Between their loved homes and the [government's] desolation!
> Blest with vict'ry and peace, may the heav'n rescued land
> *Praise* the Pow'r that hath made and *preserved* us a nation!
> Then conquer we must, when our cause it is just,
> And this be our motto: "In God is our trust!"

Our cause is just. If we will unite as a people, if we will teach our children, if we will be a people deserving of freedom:

> [Then] the star-spangled banner in triumph shall wave
> O'er the land of the free and the home of the brave!

May it ever be so.

CONCLUSION

DESPITE WHAT WE HEAR IN the news and despite what we see on television, America still represents, for all the peoples of the world, the deep-seated, unconquerable human longing to be free. If we who live in this hallowed land fail in our duty to uphold the Constitution and the natural rights protected therein, we will have allowed the greatest light and hope for liberty this world has ever known to be extinguished.

This book and others like it are a call to "arms". The threats to our freedoms and to the principles America was founded upon are very, very real. We cannot passively and without resistance, allow the government or a misguided citizenry to destroy all that we hold dear.

America's government has changed since its founding. Our nation is off course, and our freedoms are being tossed about and are drowning in the merciless waves of tyranny. We must rescue them. We must wield the peaceful sword of freedom and rally 'round the banner of liberty. We do so by educating ourselves and our children, raising our voices, insisting on responsible, ethical action from our governmental leaders, and living within our means. We must also exercise our rights, be active participants in government, become self-reliant, return to virtue, and realize our reliance upon nature's God. We cannot preserve the America of our grandfathers otherwise. We must not fail. We must not fail.

For those to whom these sentiments ring true, I encourage you to please learn more. Many of the references used as sources for this work, especially *The 5000 Year Leap* and Thomas Paine's *Common Sense,* are an excellent place to begin your search. A correct understanding of our founding principles and the corresponding commitment and courage among the rising generation is our only hope.

We must all join in the effort. We *must* save America, One Child at a Time.

May you and your contemporaries...preserve inviolate [the] Constitution, which, cherished in all its chastity and purity, will prove in the end a blessing to all the nations of the earth. - Thomas Jefferson

Sources

Allison, Andrew M., Jay A. Parry, and W. Cleon Skousen. *The Real George Washington: The True Story of America's Most Indispensible Man*. United States of America: National Center for Constitutional Studies, 1991.

Allison, Andrew M., Jay A. Parry, and W. Cleon Skousen. *The Real Benjamin Franklin: The True Story of America's Greatest Diplomat*. United States of America: National Center for Constitutional Studies, 1991.

Allison, Andrew M., Jay A. Parry, and W. Cleon Skousen. *The Real Thomas Jefferson: The True Story of America's Philosopher of Freedom*. United States of America: National Center for Constitutional Studies, 1991.

"Another Bright Idea: New Light Bulbs Can Poison You." *WorldNetDaily*, Posted February 26, 2008. http://www.wnd.com/index.php?fa=PAGE. view&pageId=57426. Retrieved July 2, 2009.

Appleby, Joyce (introduction and notes). *Common Sense and Other Writings by Thomas Paine*. New York: Barnes & Noble Books, 2005.

Beck, Glenn. *Glenn Beck's Common Sense: The Case Against an Out-of-Control Government, Inspired by Thomas Paine*. New York: Threshold Editions, 2009.

Benson, Ezra Taft. *God, Family, Country: Our Three Great Loyalties*. Salt Lake City, UT: Deseret Book Company, 1974.

Benson, Ezra Taft. *The Constitution: A Heavenly Banner*. Salt Lake City: Deseret Book Company, 1986.

Carlyle, Katy. "Farmington School Principal Apologizes for Obama 'I Pledge' Video." *Fox 13 Now Utah*, Posted September 2, 2009. http:// www.fox13now.com/news/kstu-obama-video-reaction,0,4004766.story. Retrieved September 7, 2009.

Goldberg, Jonah. *Liberal Fascism: The Secret History of the American Left, From Mussolini to the Politics of Change.* New York: Doubleday, 2007.

Gross, Grant. "Obama Includes Broadband, Smart Grid in Stimulus Package." *IDG News Service,* Posted January 8, 2009. http://www.itworld.com/government/60362/obama-includes-broadband-smart-grid-stimulus-package. Retrieved June 5, 2009.

Holland, Jeffery. "A Prayer for the Children." *The Church of Jesus Christ of Latter Day Saints.* http://www.lds.org/ldsorg/v/index.jsp?hideNav=1&locale=0&sourceId=a79874536cf0c010VgnVCM1000004d82620a____&vgnextoid=2354fccf2b7db010VgnVCM1000004d82620aRCRD. Retrieved October 25, 2009.

http://commdocs.house.gov/committees/ways/hwmw105-15.000/hwmw105-15_0f.htm. Retrieved June 12, 2009.

http://www.ed.gov/teachers/how/lessons/prek-6.pdf. Menu of Classroom Activities President Obama's Address to Students Across America (PreK-6). Retrieved September 7, 2009.

http://www.ed.gov/teachers/how/lessons/7-12.pdf. Menu of Classroom Activities President Obama's Address to Students Across America (PreK-6). Retrieved September 7, 2009.

http://www.marksquotes.com/Founding-Fathers/Adams/. Retrieved June 16, 2009.

http://www.marksquotes.com/Founding-Fathers/Hamilton/. Retrieved June 16, 2009.

http://www.marksquotes.com/Founding-Fathers/Madison/. Retrieved June 16, 2009.

http://www.marksquotes.com/Founding-Fathers/Paine/. Retrieved June 16, 2009.

http://uspolitics.about.com/od/usgovernment/a/oaths_of_office_3.htm. Retrieved September 7, 2009.

http://www.whitehouse.gov/mediaresources/. The President's Back-To-School Message to America's Students. Retrieved September 7, 2009

Kesler, Charles R. and Clinton Rossiter, eds. *The Federalist Papers.* New York: New American Library, 1999.

Kupchan, Charles A. *The End of the American Era: U. S. Foreign Policy and the Geopolitics of the Twenty-First Century*. New York: Alfred A. Knopp, 2002.

Lee, Jean B. *The Price of Nationhood: The American Revolution in Charles County*. New York: W. W. Norton & Company, 1994.

Levin, Mark R. *Liberty and Tyranny: A Conservative Manifesto*. New York: Threshold Editions, 2009.

Limbaugh, Rush H. Jr. *The Americans Who Risked Everything*. http://www. rushlimbaugh.com/home/folder/american_who_risked_everything_1. guest.html. Retrieved May 17, 2009.

Pestritto, Ronald J. and William J. Atto, eds. *American Progressivism: A Reader*. Lanham, MD: Lexington, 2008.

Phillips, Donald T. *The Founding Fathers on Leadership: Classic Teamwork in Changing Times*. New York: Warner Books, 1997.

"S.C. Governor Ordered to Take Stimulus Money." *MSNBC*, Posted June 4, 2009. http://www.msnbc.msn.com/id/31113358. Retrieved June 16, 2009.

Seligman, Martin E. P., Karen Reivich, Lisa Jaycox, and Jane Gillham. *The Optimistic Child: A Proven Program to Safeguard Children Against Depression and Build Lifelong Resilience*. New York: Houghton Mifflin Company, 1995.

Skousen, W. Cleon. *The 5000 Year Leap: The 28 Great Ideas that Changed the World*. United States of America: National Center for Constitutional Studies, 1981.

Tocqueville, Alexis de. Gerald E. Bevin (trans.), and Isaac Kramnick (introduction and notes). *Democracy in America and Two Essays on America*. New York: Penguin Books, 2003.

Tumulty, Karen. "Obama's Campaign on Health Care: Papering Over the Details." *Time*, Posted June 12, 2009. http://www.time.com/time/nation/article/0,8599,1904312,00.html. Retrieved July, 7, 2009.

Ulrich, Laurel Thatcher. *A Midwife's Tale: The Life of Martha Ballard, Based on Her Diary, 1785-1812*. New York: Vintage Books, 1990.

6735217R0

Made in the USA
Lexington, KY
15 September 2010